Behind the Scenes at
Time Team

Behind the Scenes at
Time Team

Tim Taylor

Photographs by

Chris Bennett

Dedicated to Katie T. and Les and Joan Taylor.

First published in 1998 by Channel 4 Books
This edition published 2000 by Channel 4 Books
an imprint of Macmillan Publishers Ltd,
25 Eccleston Place, London SW1W 9NF
Basingstoke and Oxford

www.macmillan.co.uk

Associated companies throughout the world.

ISBN 0 7522 7226 8

Design by DW Design
Line illustrations by Victor Ambrus

All photographs were shot with Nikon F4S and F90X cameras, fitted with Nikkor lenses
ranging from 16mm to 300mm, and on Kodak Elitechrome film stock.
Processed in London by Sky Photographic.

Colour reproduction by Aylesbury Studios Limited
Printed in Italy by New Interlitho S.P.A.

The section on scheduling on page 22 is taken from the leaflet *Scheduling Monuments*
produced by English Heritage in 1997.

This book accompanies the television series *Time Team* made by Videotext Communications
in association with Picture House Television Company for Channel 4.
Series Producer: Tim Taylor
Executive Producer: Philip Clarke

Contents

Introduction

Time Team, Channel 4's award-winning series on archaeology has completed over forty programmes. Each one was a struggle to unlock the secrets of the past in just three days; and each one contributed unique information to the historical record.

During the six years that I and other members of the *Time Team* have been working on the series, we have repeatedly been asked about what goes on behind the scenes. Does it really take three days? Is Tony Robinson interested in archaeology? What was our most exciting find? How do we choose the sites?

This book answers these questions and others, and provides an insight into what happens behind the scenes of Britain's most popular archaeological programme. The photographer, Chris Bennett, was given unique access to all the stages of the production process from the initial choice of sites, through research and filming to the final stages of post-production. Chris, who has worked on many 'behind the scenes' books on subjects ranging from the Red Arrows to the famous Harrods store in Knightsbridge, describes this access as 'exceptional'. It meant he was able to get the kind of candid shots that reflect the tensions and drama that inevitably result when a team of more than fifty people battles for three days with the often intractable secrets of the past.

Each of the sites selected for *Behind the Scenes at Time Team* created its own particular challenges, both in terms of the research and background material needed to bring a specific historical period to light, and in the archaeological techniques used to locate the evidence.

Historically the book ranges from prehistory to the more recent past. A Palaeolithic cave, Josiah Wedgwood's first pottery factory, ironworks for the Roman fleet, a lost dockyard used by Henry V's navy and a bomber that crashed in the Second World War provide the main stories.

The environmental and working conditions for each site presented different challenges. We struggled in the depths of an underground tunnel and searched a vast area of landscape in the rolling Sussex countryside. We were up to our ears in tarmac, concrete and bricks in the middle of a town, and coped with unexploded munitions on an environmentally sensitive site in the Norfolk marshes.

Each site required different archaeological techniques and these are described in detail, along with the thinking behind the strategies we followed. In any creative process there are tensions between opposing elements. These are necessary and on *Time Team* we have to find a balance between the realities of an archaeological dig and making a film with a strong story line.

Tension can surface most obviously as we move towards the end of a shoot, when we are often faced with a decision as to whether or not more trenches should be opened on the third day. The last few trenches have often held the key to a site and I have to try to get more work done on the final day if I believe this might answer the critical question that the programme and archaeology are asking. However, I also have to respect the archaeologists' need to ensure that whatever we do can be properly recorded and excavated in the time we have left. From the start I have had an unwritten agreement with Mick Aston that I will not push the archaeology beyond the point where he feels comfortable. On the other hand, both he and Phil Harding realize that I sometimes have to ask them to go further than the more conservative members of their profession might go. Having a good enough relationship with each other to achieve this balance is important and a critical part of my job. A recent shoot provided an illustration of this.

By the middle of the final day at the 1998 live shoot at Bawsey in Suffolk we had very little concrete evidence for dating some of the major features. Mick and the other archaeologists were reluctant to open up more trenches, but by arguing the case and showing them the latest geophysics we were able to agree on two final trenches. These turned out to be crucial to our understanding of the site. In one we found dating evidence, including a beautiful loom weight, from the Anglo-Saxon period which at last gave us a date for the huge ditch that surrounded the site. In the other we uncovered an important set of Anglo-Saxon kilns that will prove vital to the future interpretation of what was happening at Bawsey 1,500 years ago. Without this information the site and the programme would have been poorer.

On the other hand, with my archaeological hat on I also have to ensure that the process of getting a programme made does not distort the archaeological reality. This can mean that the story line in a script that has been worked on and researched for weeks may have to be abandoned or I have to help by pushing directors down an entirely new path. If this does not happen I always feel that we must be going down a line that is too predictable. A viewer told us that he had overheard a group of students laying bets with each other on whether *Time Team* would find anything in that evening's programme, and it would be nice if this story were true. For me, pursuing the honesty of that uncertainty has been an important element in what makes the series work. It is why the programme is unique on television and I would like to think that this is one of the reasons for *Time Team*'s success.

Time Team has always faced the prospect of failure; we test a hypothesis and sometimes we get it wrong and have to think again. As usual, the sites described here took us on a roller-coaster ride from fear of failure to hopes of final success. *Time Team* is archaeology as it happens and I hope this book will enable you to share the traumas and struggle behind the cameras – the other half of the story that you don't always see in the final cut.

The Beginning

Time Team started with a book and a conversation. The book, left at my house by some friends, was *Fieldwork in Local History* by W.G. Hoskins. Its theme – that the landscape can be 'read' and that this reveals the past – fascinated me. So did Hoskins' readable style and his ability to introduce an interpretation of the landscape that brings it alive so that it can be appreciated by non-experts. At about this time a reservoir was being built in a valley to the north of Dartmoor. This involved flooding many ancient farm sites but before they were destroyed archaeologists would have the chance to uncover their early origins. Researchers in the area had for some time been convinced that the sites might go back to the Saxon period and earlier, but modern-day occupation and the tendency to convert ancient barns into dwellings meant that few had been excavated to any depth. I wrote a brief outline for a programme and sent it to Channel 4. The idea of a reservoir slowly filling with water, as excavators battled to find out what they could from sites that were gradually disappearing, seemed to strike a note with Sue Shepherd, the commissioning editor who commissioned three programmes.

With the help of Simon Timms, Devon county archaeologist, I began to work on the series, which was eventually called *Time Signs*. Simon introduced me to Mick Aston from the University of Bristol, and Mick in turn suggested Phil Harding to do some reconstruction archaeology. I had wanted to re-create some aspects of prehistoric life in the valley – the origin of the *Time Team* reconstructions or 'cameos' – and Phil showed us how to fell trees with a flint axe, create fire with a bow drill and make and shoot an arrow. I have fond memories of one of my first meetings with Phil. I had brought him down to the valley to demonstrate the use of a flint axe. We needed to film a sequence showing how prehistoric people cleared the forests. With camera rolling and amid an air of tense expectation Phil stepped up to a tree, swung his axe and delivered a mighty blow – only for the axe-head to drop out of the shaft. I think this was the first occasion on which I heard the immortal words 'Oh bugger!'. It became clear over the following months that despite the occasional mishap, Phil was not only a genius

Opposite: *Professor Mick Aston meditating on the likely identity of an archaeological artefact – in this case a ship's nail. The striped pullover is standard Aston apparel.*

in the area of flint knapping but was also prepared to have a go at a variety of ancient techniques in front of the camera.

Phil's skills and easy manner had an obvious appeal, and it was clear to me that Mick was a great communicator of archaeology. He described me as one of the few 'television people' – a derisive term in Mick's vocabulary – he could get on with and someone who, in addition, was prepared to read enough background material to understand what he was talking about. A friendship began.

Over a year and a half Phil, Mick and I traipsed up and down muddy valleys and helped to carry cameras and sound gear. Initially our cameraman was Bernard Hedges. Limited budgets and the need to record developments on the site at short notice meant that I was also doing camera work, and for the later programmes Bernard and I were joined by Nick Dance. Nick was to become the senior *Time Team* cameraman and his style of shooting, which reflects the way I want to capture archaeology 'as it happens', is a distinctive element in the series.

Opposite: Anyone who has worked on Time Team *knows it is an enjoyable experience – if hard work. Sue Francis agreed to help out with a cameo by rolling wool on her thighs. Damian Goodburn and Phil took a professional interest in the process.*

Above: Victor Ambrus draws a picture of what the site may have looked like in the past. His drawings always prove a great attraction to the viewers and the local people. His ability to re-create the past in a short space of time under difficult circumstances is a unique skill that is a vital element in the programme.

Above: *A typical place for a* Time Team *chat: around the bonnet of the Discovery. Nick Dance films Tony and Mick in conference with the experts.*

He is excellent at capturing the action and being in the right place to follow its thread. When we work with archaeologists, who are not actors, we have to get spontaneous reactions where possible, and capture the feel of a live-action sequence. Some cameramen shoot in short takes which need to be assembled in the editing suite with a lot of edits and cutaways, and the end result tends to feel less 'realistic'. With Nick and all the regular *Time Team* camera crews we try to capture the flow of an event. It was a piece of luck to meet Nick as early as I did.

The conversation that inspired the *Time Team* series was with Mick. As the filming of *Time Signs* progressed he and I began to enjoy discussing archaeology and after one filming day, wet, tired and in need of a cup of tea, we were chatting in a service station on the edge of the A30 near Dartmoor. Mick told me how he and a friend had missed a bus somewhere in the Midlands and spent an enjoyable hour waiting for the next one by mapping out the medieval streets of the town. My reaction was that if they could do that in an hour, how much more could be done in three days? *Time Team* was under way. Over the following six months

I put together different variations on the theme and included a 'cameo' reconstruction element.

Developing an initial idea into a successful television format requires a lot of hard work and trial and error. I wanted to put together a team of people with the right chemistry and set of ideas to carry the viewer along. Drawings by Victor Ambrus, whose illustrations had caught my eye in a second-hand Reader's Digest book on history, were included. With the introduction of an incident room, the historical reconstructions and the history sequences, that found their natural presenter in Robin Bush, the key features of the series were in place. At some point in the past Mick had held a course on archaeology in Greece which had been attended by one Tony Robinson, and Tony's interest in the subject and his connection with Mick made him an obvious choice for presenter. As a result of his experience in television he would also be a valuable source of advice as the series progressed. During a recent conversation with him he told me that nowadays more people come up and talk to him about his *Time Team* work than refer to his role as Baldrick in *Blackadder*.

An interesting element of the programme style is that from the beginning we decided that only Tony should address the camera: it is a television convention that viewers like to have just one person talking to them. Mick had done a great job in this role on *Time Signs* but he had to change his way of getting information across for *Time Team*. His good relationship with Tony was important in achieving the right chemistry. Tony could play the grit in the archaeological oyster and ask questions the viewers would like to ask. He would also be able to spot archaeological prevarications and generally keep the team on their toes. Field archaeologist Carenza Lewis completed the original team, joining us after the pilot.

After a year's wait due to changes in personnel at Channel 4 – 'You'll have to wait and see what the next commissioning editor thinks' – *Time Team* was under way. Karen Brown, our new commissioning editor, recognized its potential even though it was based

Above: *Somewhere in an English field, John, as on many occasions, explains the details of the geophysics results. Geophysics has become a crucial element of Time Team.*

on a subject that not many people would have thought of as popular viewing material, and the idea was presented to her by a producer who did not exactly have a typical television background.

In the waiting period *Time Team* had a brief existence as a spin-off – a sort of 'spot the object' game show complete with spinning panels – but it was always clear that the basic idea was strong and that, as *Time Signs* had shown, there was an audience for archaeology. The series had two other allies at Channel 4: John Willis and Andrea Wonfor who kept the idea alive while we waited for Karen Brown to take up her post.

From the start I wanted *Time Team* to be different from other history and archaeology programmes on television. I had watched many *Chronicles* and other history/archaeology programmes over the years and often enjoyed them, but I was suspicious of what I felt was a 'talking head' style combined with a sense of experts talking down to the audience. I knew real archaeology was about testing a hypothesis and often finding out that your initial guess was incorrect. I wanted a group of people who would take risks and get it wrong and still be able to keep going. I believed this would keep the programme always fresh.

It is to the great credit of all the team members that they were prepared to risk this approach when they were still uncertain whether or not *Time Team* would be accepted by their peers. They are among the rare group of archaeologists who have been prepared to stick their heads over the parapet to make the subject more popular to the general public. The extent of that popularity can be measured by the millions who watch the programme, and by other factors including the estimated fifteen per cent increase in applications to study archaeology at university, which many admissions tutors put down to *Time Team*'s influence. We have also received tremendous support and acceptance from the archaeological community and been awarded the British Archaeological Award for Best Archaeological Programme twice in a row. It is this kind of recognition that has helped to encourage our archaeologists.

Eight years after that first series went out, one of my great pleasures has been to remind Mick at regular intervals of his final words to me – the words of a good old Brummie cynic – when we parted at the service station after that initial conversation: 'It'll never happen Tim – it'll never happen.'

Below: The directors on Time Team *have to be flexible and cope with sudden changes to the script. It is my job to keep them aware of the likely direction the archaeology is going. Here Simon Raikes and I are discussing our strategy on Day Two of the Cheddar shoot.*

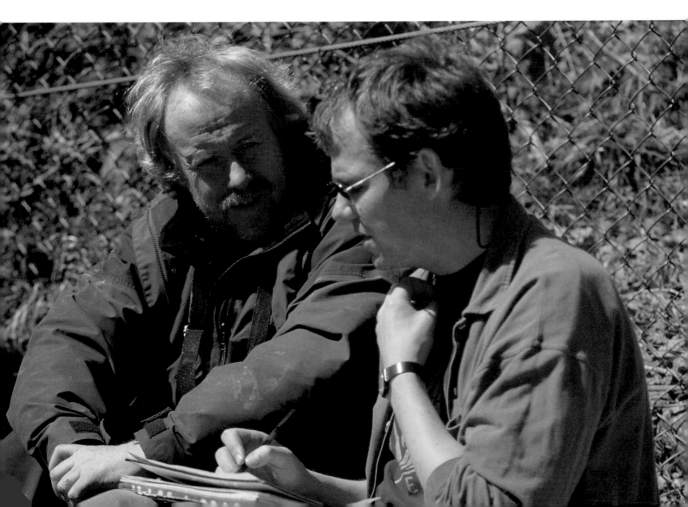

Who's Who

Tony Robinson, the series presenter, is best known for his role as Baldrick in *Blackadder* and as the Sheriff of Nottingham in *Maid Marian and Her Merry Men*, which he also wrote. He has a keen interest in history and archaeology – he is president of the Young Archaeologists' Club – and is particularly fascinated by ancient Greece and the biblical lands of the Middle East.

Professor Mick Aston, the team leader, has been involved with archaeology for more than thirty years, and is currently Professor of Landscape Archaeology at the University of Bristol. He has written numerous articles and books, including *Interpreting the Landscape*, the standard work on landscape archaeology.

Phil Harding works as a field archaeologist with Wessex Archaeology, and has been involved in a project listing and plotting all known Palaeolithic sites in Britain. He has also completed a number of excavation reports – including some for *Time Team* – on sites ranging from the Palaeolithic to the Industrial Revolution. He continues to demonstrate flint knapping at craft shows and to local societies.

Carenza Lewis has been with the Royal Commission on the Historical Monuments of England (RCHME) since 1985. A specialist in the medieval period and in historic landscapes, she worked extensively as a field archaeologist in Wessex and co-edited a collection of essays on the medieval landscape of this area; she is now based in Cambridge. Her book on the medieval landscape of the East Midlands – *Village, Hamlet and Field* – was published in 1997.

Victor Ambrus, who arrived in Britain from Hungary in 1956, is a freelance illustrator with almost 300 books to his credit. Winner of the World Wildlife Award and twice winner of the Kate Greenaway gold medal for the best illustrated book of the year, his recent work includes illustrated editions of *The Iliad* and *Moby Dick* and a book on the Anglo-Saxon ship burials at Sutton Hoo. He is a Fellow of the Royal Society of Arts and the Royal Society of Engravers.

Robin Bush, formerly deputy county archivist for Somerset, is a freelance lecturer, historian and broadcaster. An expert in genealogy and on the history of early emigration to the United States, he is the author of numerous books on local history, including a definitive guide to Somerset.

Stewart Ainsworth trained as a surveyor before moving into the archaeology section of the Ordnance Survey Department as an investigator, working in Britain on archaeological sites and monuments and, on secondment, on a mapping project on the Caribbean islands of St Kitts and Nevis. In 1985 he joined the Royal Commission on the Historical Monuments of England as an archaeological investigator and is now head of the field archaeology office for the West Midlands. Along with Bernard Thomason he is responsible for what we call the 'lumps and bumps'.

Bernard Thomason first worked in archaeology in 1972, as an air-photograph interpreter at Cambridge University. In 1980 he began working with the Royal Commission on the Historical Monuments of England as an archaeological illustrator. Since then he has been employed as an architectural surveyor and illustrator. He specializes in producing technical solutions to surveying and illustration, and is Head of Technical Survey for Archaeology at the RCHME.

John Gater has been involved in archaeological geophysics for almost twenty years, working for British Gas, the Ancient Monuments Laboratory (English Heritage) and Bradford University Research. In 1986 he set up GSB Prospection, an independent consultancy in geophysics for archaeology. He is also an associate editor of the *Journal of Archaeological Prospection*.

Dr Chris Gaffney has worked in geophysics since 1983, including extensive site-based experience in the United Kingdom, Greece and the former Yugoslavia. In 1989 he formed a partnership with John Gater at GSB Prospection. He too is an associate editor of the *Journal of Archaeological Prospection*.

Creative TV is responsible for *Time Team*'s computer graphics. **Sue Francis** worked with the BBC for two years and as a freelance designer before, in 1989, setting up Creative TV Facilities where she is chief designer. **Steve Breeze** was signed to RCA Records as a singer/songwriter before joining Creative TV where he creates three-dimensional visualizations.

The Production Process

Each series of *Time Team* begins with a huge pile of letters – we get more than a thousand a year – from members of the public, special interest groups concerned with protecting our history and, increasingly, archaeologists. We also have an idea of the kinds of sites we would like to go to because they have not appeared in previous series. Gradually a few start to establish themselves. Researchers reduce the pile by eliminating the weakest or frankly potty suggestions and begin to discuss sites that appear to be possible with people like county archaeologists.

I am often asked which kind of proposals make it through the system and which don't. The answer is partly the obvious one; that a letter accompanied by good drawings and photographs, and with some solidly researched archaeological content, is more likely to be accepted. Sending us bits of supposed archaeological material is not a good idea. In the past we have received interesting Roman necklaces that turned out to be lavatory chains and pieces of gravel that the punter was convinced bore the faces of Roman emperors.

It is very useful for us to know exactly who owns the land. Many great ideas fall by the wayside because we can't be sure that the landowner will allow us access. Often the research team will consider a relatively simple idea that has some good artefact evidence checked by a local archaeologist. In the 1998 filming year we carried out an excavation in a back garden in Papcastle, Cumbria. A family had uncovered a large number of Roman finds while building a patio there. They had made a careful inventory of their finds, got the local

archaeologist and museum to confirm that they were Roman and then sent us a letter complete with photographs of the site. This one belongs to a group we refer to as 'back garden punter' sites – a 'punter' is the name we give to a person who suggests we come to a site in the first place. We like to have at least some of this sort of punter in each series.

It is amazing how many people uncover important archaeology in their back gardens. The millions of gardeners happily planting their borders are potentially the largest group of field walkers we have. It is also surprising that so many of them discover finds which they feel won't be of interest to their museum or local archaeologists, but then decide to tell *Time Team* about them.

We are always on the lookout for places that viewers would not normally connect with archaeology, and like to have a variety of historical periods and archaeological environments. There is also an element of serendipity and experience. After forty programmes I have come to trust my instinct that a site is right and tend to follow my hunches. However, I am reluctant to go ahead if Mick, who is a useful source of contacts and ideas, has a strong reason for being against a site. Tony is kept informed of the kind of areas we are looking at and so are Channel 4 and Philip Clarke, the executive producer. An executive producer's job is to act as a sort of *éminence grise*, keeping an eye on both the administration of the programme and the direction it is taking. Any small company that comes up with a potentially successful idea tends to get pushed in the direction of a good executive producer, and Philip became involved with *Time Team* from Series 2 onwards.

A major part of my job is to make sure the right sites are selected. The choice tends to be my final decision – which can be a bit nerve-racking at times.

County archaeologists are one of our key groups of contacts. We have good contacts in most areas of the country and this has created an important network, which acts as a reference point when we begin to look for new sites. Our access to a site is often based on our ability to provide resources that would not otherwise be available. Geophysics is particularly useful and we often use it over a larger area than is actually necessary in order to supply data for local archaeologists. In Navan, County Armagh in Northern Ireland, they are still processing the work that the geophysics team did two years ago and excavating areas of interest based on the data.

Opposite: Now I have worked with him for several years, Phil Harding occasionally allows me to have the odd scrape. Getting as close as possible to the archaeological reality is an important part of my role as producer – at least that's what I tell Phil.

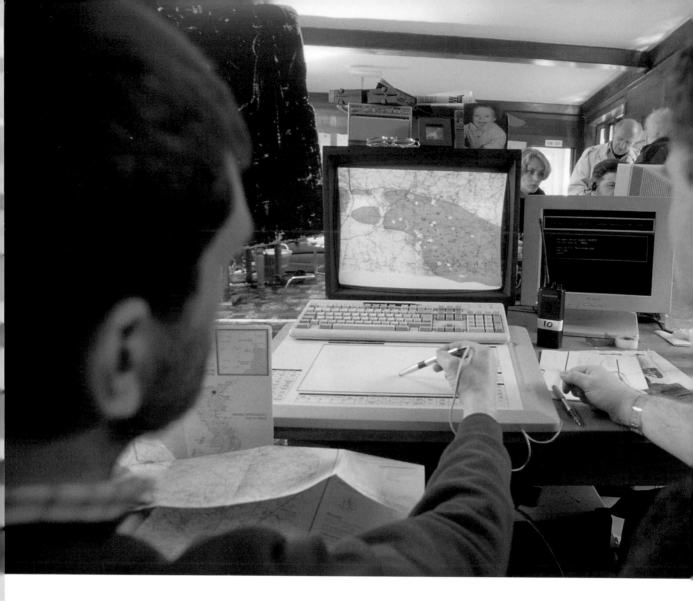

Above: *In the incident room. Stewart Ainsworth uses the computer to sort out the landscape.*

It is important that this information is made available to archaeologists in general and that our work is accurately recorded, particularly with regard to the position of the trenches. Bernard and Stewart use a Leica Global Positioning System (GPS) which relies on information beamed down by a constellation of twenty-four satellites belonging to the United States Department of Defense. These orbit constantly around the earth and signals can be received from at least four of them at any time of the day or night. By using sensitive equipment that can receive and decode the signals it is possible to get a very accurate three-dimensional fix anywhere in the world. With this technique trenches, geophysics grids, environmental bore-holes and field-walking can be accurately located on a map. GPS equipment

Behind the Scenes at *Time Team*

also enables Bernard and Stewart to record three-dimensional points and computerize them to create landscape models and a picture of what the site originally looked like. I am always amazed at how accurate the system is. It can locate a point in plan within three centimetres (1¼ inches) anywhere on the earth's surface. Theoretically a teacup outlined on one of our sites in Britain could be paid a visit by a missile flown from another continent.

Bernard makes a complete computerized record of the trenches and finds and our resident digging team also records trenches with a theodolite. Each key trench-level is drawn by hand using a grid suspended over the surface. Hand drawings are uniquely accurate recordings of a surface and are preferred to photographs.

The final question county archaeologists usually raise is: 'What about post-excavation and who'll make good?' Post-excavation covers a wide range of activities including writing up reports, processing finds and making sure the site is tidy and safe after we leave. On some shoots we have hundreds of finds to process. This includes cleaning, categorizing and, in the case of the more fragile ones, conserving them. Costs for this can run into thousands of pounds which might explain the somewhat ambiguous attitude I occasionally have to heaps of finds coming out of the trenches. A significant Anglo-Saxon burial with bones, grave goods and other artefacts could produce a bill in excess of £4,000 or £5,000 in the post-excavation stage. This has to be allowed for in the overall budget for a series.

An important part of the early stage of production is locating the incident room. This is where we have the computer equipment, books and maps and where we process finds. We also try to give Sue Francis and Steve Breeze an idea of the kind of structures they will be re-creating with their computer graphics, and let Victor know which historical period he needs to think about in advance. Victor's experience and skill mean he is able to give us an accurate drawing of a typical Saxon hut or medieval castle in a relatively short space of time. His

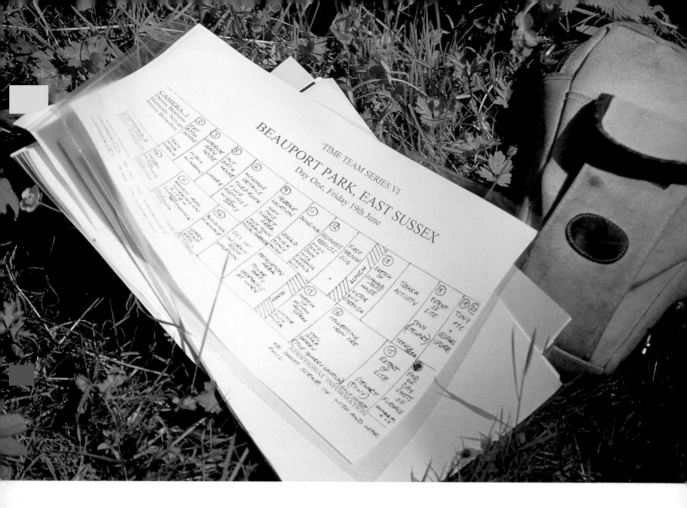

Schedule document shown in photograph reads:

TIME TEAM SERIES VI

BEAUPORT PARK, EAST SUSSEX

Day One, Friday 19th June

Above: *After the script is finished, each day's shooting is mapped out on a schedule. This tells the* Time Team *who is filming what, where and when. After a hard day's filming the director has to work on a new one for the next day so they're not always as neat as this.*

drawings are always a great attraction for the local punters and viewers alike and, combined with Sue's reconstructions of objects and Steve's three-dimensional buildings and landscapes, form a critical element of a programme.

Before a *Time Team* dig takes place we come to an agreement with the community as to where to send the finds. Often this is to the local museum. Landowners theoretically have the right of ownership but we usually persuade them to pass on any finds to an appropriate local body who will care for them. Any gold or silver object that has been hidden and whose owner is unknown is covered by the law of treasure-trove: it belongs to the Crown and is subject to an inquest at a coroner's court to establish the circumstances of its loss or deposition. Archaeologists frequently give evidence to such inquests. The person who has found the object is often allowed to keep it – or an institution like the British Museum may buy it for their collection.

Throughout this process Ella Galinski and Tory Batten, the assistant producers, make sure the archaeological story and programme narrative are accurate and that we are establishing good links with the community and experts. With so much investment of energy and money going into just three days it is critical that they – and the whole team – have a complete understanding of what we will be doing and that this is how the director sees the programme going. They work with the director on the likely route of the archaeology and it is then up to them and the researchers to visualize how the three days will be shot and produce a shooting script. The script includes details of Tony's pieces to camera and the order in which scenes will appear. It allocates a series of events to each of the main days and divides the presentation of the material between the various *Time Team* members. This document and the research design form the basis of a production meeting held a couple of weeks before the shoot, which is attended by everyone involved in the programme and enables us to get feed-back from the *Time Team*, Tony and the rest of the production team.

Below: Phil gets the chance to drink his favourite drink from a somewhat classier container than his usual pint glass.

CHAPTER 1

Cooper's Hole, Cheddar

TONY'S PIECE TO CAMERA: 'It may not look very comfortable, but before huts and houses this was home. In fact, this cave in the Cheddar Gorge could be one of the oldest homes in the country. Between five and ten thousand years ago families of Stone Age hunter-gatherers, the cavemen of legend, probably used this cave as a place to eat, sleep, shelter, and ... do whatever else they did. But to find whatever they left behind is going to be a huge task. Thousands of years of rainfall have washed tons and tons of mud into this cave, and washed much of the evidence deep into the tunnels at the back ... if we're going to find anything at all we're going to have to dig a long way down that way (*points down*), and a long way (*indicating tunnels*) that way ...'

Opposite: *Placing locating points for mapping the cave interior was an important element of ensuring that the finds and our trenches could be accurately located.*

Above: *Gathered together on the first day, Dr Larry Barham and Dr Kate Robson-Brown discuss tactics with Phil and Carenza.*

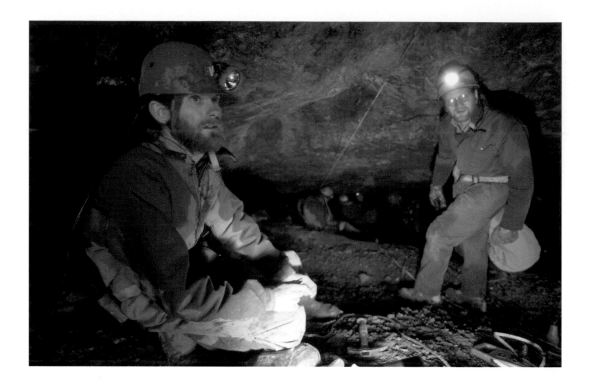

Above: *Mick Worthington and Stewart Ainsworth put in place the rest of a grid to locate our work in Cooper's Hole. As more diggers began to work at depth we became aware that the air quality had to be carefully monitored.*

for archaeological evidence was to some extent understandable – their main focus was to locate underground passages and if possible discover the great Cheddar underwater river – a Holy Grail for most Somerset cavers. They would be invaluable on the *Time Team* dig, not only for their previous experience of the site but also for their skill at caving. Our main contact was Malcolm Cotter who is now in his sixties. It would be up to us to ensure that the cavers, like everyone on the team, appreciated the stringent archaeological standards we would be working under.

Archaeological sites that might not otherwise be excavated or that have been neglected seem to fit in with the *Time Team* way of working and Cooper's Hole seemed badly in need of adoption by somebody. The irony was that as soon as we began to take an interest we were faced with an archaeological fifth degree as to our intentions. Meetings at various universities followed during which I emphasized that our working practice would follow the guidelines laid out by experts in cave excavation, and that all necessary care would be taken to sample the areas of Cooper's Hole that needed sampling.

Palaeolithic archaeologists have too many painful memories in their collective consciousness of caves destroyed by excessive and careless excavation in the past, and have become ultra-sensitive to the methods used to tease out evidence. It is critical, for instance, that a grid is suspended above the cave floor so that finds can be precisely located. It is also vital to follow a sampling strategy that allows archaeologists to identify an exact level for each of the various pieces of evidence, some of which may be as small as a grain of pollen.

My first contact with the palaeontologists with whom we would eventually work was at Bristol University. They had kindly offered the

Following page: Overlooking the entrance to Cooper's Hole we took the opportunity to talk to the cavers about their earlier experiences of the site. The precarious location caused me concern and I was relieved when the filming was completed.

Team Profile

Steve Shearn – *Sound Recordist*

'Cheddar was an unforgettable shoot because it took me weeks to clean the mud off my cables afterwards. The location was a very familiar scene to me as I had been in and out of caves while working on the *999* series and enjoy caving as a hobby. This one was particularly taxing because of the wet and muddy conditions outside, as well as inside, the cave.

'I came to sound recording when, as a young musician, I began writing material for a BBC arts magazine programme. It was here that I met Clive North, who needed someone to do the news. I went round to his house and he gave me a quick introduction to the equipment. The following week the material I had recorded was broadcast!

'I had a good feeling from the very first take of *Time Team*. I have only missed four programmes and three of these were due to a broken leg. My two favourite shoots would be Islay, Scotland because it was such an unpredictable place and Sanday on Orkney where the light was fantastic. The worst *Time Team* was Richmond because the dig was underneath a flight path with only forty seconds between planes. Aircraft are very difficult to cut out as they are on the same frequency as the voice. Everything had to be recorded in very short takes, and cut in the edit suite.

'The biggest task is recording large groups of people on the move. This involves me stumbling around attached to the camera while trying to ensure a good sound is recorded. Having a healthy working relationship with your fellow crew members is essential as you never know who is going to speak next, so you just have to go with the flow.'

opening piece to camera (PTC). What will we hang our story line on? It is a bit like nailing your colours to the mast. Tony says something like, '*Time Team* has got just three days to find "X".' Critical threads of the script hang on this and it commits us to ascertaining our line of attack. We don't like implying that we can find something when this is next to impossible. Equally, we don't like stating the obvious – the PTC has to be a challenge, a mystery, but the goal has to be attainable. What would it be for Cooper's Hole? Could we say: 'Will we find evidence of Stone Age man?' With some degree of reservation and trepidation we decided that this would be our angle. I say trepidation because I don't like Tony to carry a line like this, and feel we are selling the viewer an unachievable dream. There are too many archaeological television programmes that cynically propose a search for the lost ark or something similar, knowing there is no hope of finding it, but that it will grab the viewer's attention anyway. In the event, Tony's opening PTC stated that finding what Stone Age man left behind would be 'a huge task'.

We now had a strategy in place and after final telephone calls to Bob Croft and Lord Bath we could begin the countdown to filming. As we had all agreed that we would have to go as far as possible into the cave the cavers would be part of the team. Tony was prepared to go underground and we needed a cameraman who could cope with the technical challenge and a crew who would not mind getting muddy. Cameraman Clive North and *Time Team* sound supervisor Steve Shearn had had experience of caving and Clive had the technical know-how to ensure that we got pictures in this extreme environment. By now our researchers had come up with a chronology of events in the cave. This is a useful document for most sites and helps everyone to get a grip on what happened when.

According to at least one source a Mr Cooper was in occupation in the 1800s (apparently caves have always been popular places in which to live). Alternatively, and perhaps more likely, it was where he kept his cart – a convenient natural garage. In 1931 and 1932 excavations under R.F. Parry extended 4.5 metres (fifteen feet) into the cave and went down to 4.5 metres (fifteen feet). Parry found animal bones, layers of charcoal, an Iron Age layer and a layer of clay but possibly did not pierce the stal. Also in the 1930s, local cavers dug in the cave but found little. Bones claimed to be from the cave were donated to the Natural History Museum in 1946 and a fragment of the jaw of a red deer has recently been recorded as being from the lowest level (layer twenty) which looks

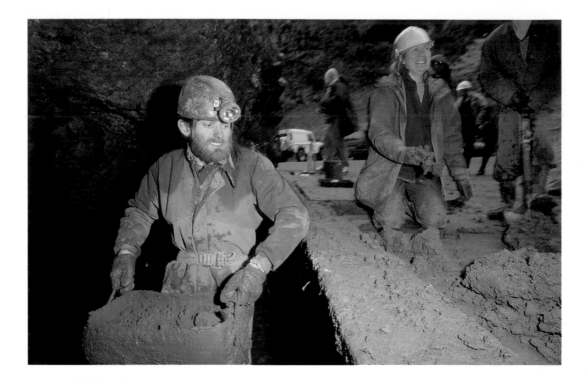

Above: *The spoil at the surface had to be heaved over the retaining wall and sorted through. This is probably one of the most physically tiring jobs our diggers have undertaken.*

like the Upper Palaeolithic material from Gough's Cave. Thirteen years later, in 1959, the Mendip Caving Group asked the Marquis of Bath for permission to excavate the site in search of a larger cave system. The cavers drew plans of their work and found bones of animals including red deer, but these could have been washed in or fallen through holes in the roof. The following year, in 1960, Lord Bath cleared the entrance and built a retaining wall. In 1961 the caving group found Iron Age bones and pottery above the stal floor; below it, a hundred feet further in and twenty-five feet down, they discovered bones, including those of horses and foxes, that the British Museum identified as dating from before the Iron Age. The caving group went down a new side passage in 1962 and found what was thought to be the skeleton of an arctic fox. This is now in the Cheddar Caves Museum and has been identified as a red-fox skeleton. In 1963 a caver found a large flint core. Severe flooding deposited mud from the road in the cave between 1966 and 1968. In the 1980s the cave roof collapsed as a result of further digging in the 'arctic fox' tunnel and blocked the passage.

At the start of Day One the rain had already begun to fall. We had known that Cooper's Hole would be a muddy site but as the first few

Team Profile

Mick Worthington – *Digger*

'When I was asked to do Cooper's Hole I was told the following: "It'll be fun digging in a cave." (Full of broken bottles I found.) "We'll provide all the right equipment." (It weighed more than me.) "It's the middle of summer." (There was a flood.) "There are only three trenches to dig." (Vertical for twenty feet, but the water only came up to my neck.) After the Orkney programme this was my favourite *Time Team* ever – hard work but fantastic fun.

'I trained initially as a mechanical engineer but soon discovered that working in factories wasn't for me, and have been in archaeology since 1984. I applied to my local museum, which was looking for people to excavate industrial materials and, with my engineering background, got the job in the archaeology department. I think my best find to date would have to be the first iron rails ever made in Coalbrookdale in 1751-52. They were important because there was no previous documented evidence.

'I specialize in dendrochronology – the chronological and environmental information contained in tree rings – and go round the country dating old buildings by calculating the age of their timbers. The most hazardous part of the job is clambering around the very top of cathedral roofs seventy to eighty feet above the ground.

'I also enjoyed Sanday in the Orkneys, because the Viking site was so fantastic and a beautiful place to visit. The archaeology, although demanding, was excellent, which added up to a good programme. My contemporaries are usually very interested in my work for the series and generally ask how I got involved in the first place! My advice to anyone thinking of a career as an archaeologist is to look into other professions first. It is very difficult to make a living from archaeology and it is perhaps better to keep it as a hobby, practised in a warm climate.

'My finest moment in archaeology so far was when I photographed a church in the middle of the Nubian desert from a kite and managed to get a perfectly composed photograph of a wonderful site. I still have the photograph, somewhere ...'

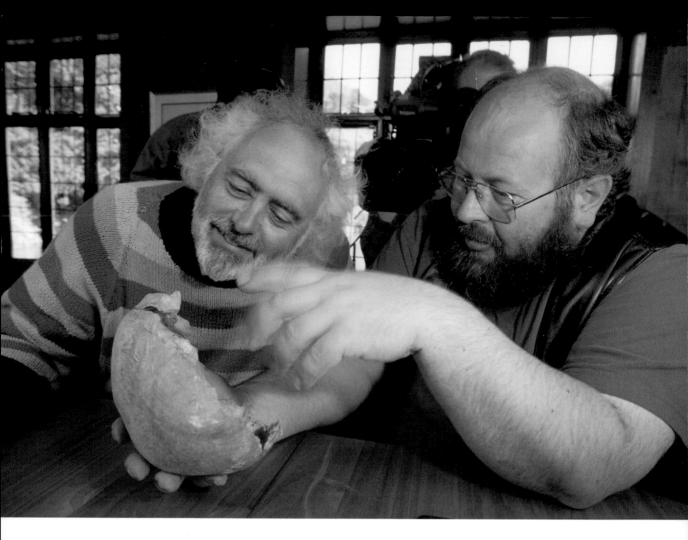

Above: *Mick and Andy Currant explore the recesses of a cave-dweller's skull. Some of the bones, according to Andy, provided evidence of cannibalism.*

hours of filming began, we started to appreciate the realities of the challenge we had taken on. A rainy month previously meant surfaces were wet and the area of the cave where the stal had been broken was collecting water. Pumps could deal with some of this sea of liquid mud, but the only way to get rid of the handfuls of more solid clay and mud spoil that needed to be cleared was for a team of diggers and cavers to act as a chain gang to carry it to the surface. Rather like an underwater version of wartime escape movies, the team gradually worked it back in improvised plastic sleds which they dragged to the surface with ropes. The disturbed mud that had been washed over the top of the spoil had to be checked for artefacts and by the end of the day we had accumulated an interesting collection of drinks cans. We tried to work out how we could use a motorized winch but this had a major drawback – fumes from any vehicle would sink into the cave and, because the air in the shaft was already depleted by the number of cavers, would present a serious danger.

Trench 1 in the car park at the mouth of the cave had been started and was clearly going to be hard going. Trench 2 was deep down on the right-hand side of the cave in a tunnel that had been penetrated by cavers in the past. The combination of JCBs and heavy, mud-covered human diggers dripping rain and liquid mud created a fairly gruesome sight at the cave entrance, and as Day One came to a close it was with some relief that I contemplated a trip to the incident room to catch up on the story there. Mick Worthington, one of our key diggers, would keep an eye on things.

Andy Currant, our expert from the Natural History Museum, was able to give us the low-down on bits of bone which we had brought . together in the incident room. He was able to elaborate on his theory that the bones in Gough's Cave a hundred yards down the road from our site showed evidence of cannibalism. One of the joys of *Time Team* is that in general we have access to the best experts going – the people who have done the most recent research and are familiar with up-to-date ideas on their subject. Andy was both an enthusiast and a great communicator. The only problem was that the longer we discussed what he had found in Gough's Cave, the more obvious the lack of evidence retrieved so far from Cooper's Hole became.

Below: *Lord Bath pays the team a visit and gets a view of the interior via our remote camera. Carenza was soon to enter the cave herself.*

depth where we might not be able to step the sides to ensure that excavation would be safe. According to safety regulations, trenches more than 1.2 metres (four feet) deep require two possible actions: shoring, sloping the sides at a forty-five degree angle, battering or stepping the sides. Substantial barriers must be erected around excavations deeper than two metres (6½ feet). Stepping simply means widening the trench so that it can be dug down in a series of steps which make the sides more stable. Shoring is a critical business and, if lives are not to be endangered, must be carried out perfectly. A frame of metal or wood is inserted in the hole and prevents the sides collapsing. A trench never seems to be the best size for the accro props – adjustable steel tubes to support the shoring – you have on hand, which can cause delays while new ones are hired and the hole is shored to everyone's satisfaction. I have stood close to trenches when they have collapsed and the sound of the falling sides and the speed at which they fall is frightening. We always err on the side of caution once a trench approaches the magic depth of 1.2 metres (four feet).

Trench 1 created a panic, but it is difficult to say why. It was definitely deep and dangerous, but we had seen similar trenches before

Opposite: *Some trenches just have an unpleasant look and this one was potentially lethal. However, we still had to measure its depth and try to record the layers prior to back-filling.*

Above: *Carefully perched near the edge of Trench 1, Dr Larry Barham points out some of the main features. After this final shot, and with recording of the main details complete, the trench was back-filled as the sides had started to collapse.*

Above: *Phil carving the hole in the bone tool. At this stage we had yet to test its possible function.*

Opposite: *Flint knapper Phil in his natural element – working away at the mouth of a cave.*

and they had not produced such an air of worry among the diggers and the team. I think it is true to say that trenches have personalities. You look at a particular hole and it looks nasty and mean – the kind of hole that would bite your leg off. This had that sort of look – a bull terrier with attitude. People would come up to me, draw me to one side and gesture at it saying, 'It's a killer.' Mick became increasingly concerned and we all felt that we did not want anyone even near the edge. As bits of rock began to fall into the trench they landed on the bottom with a solid 'thunk' and you could feel the earth shake. We decided that our last act would be to measure the depth of the trench and backfill as soon as possible. Phil with a tape measure and Richard Trainer with digital machines miraculously managed to get the same reading – much to Phil's delight – and it gave us the level of the original rock surface outside the cave at which it had been during prehistoric occupation.

With the necessary safety precautions under way I was able to enjoy the more pleasant sight of Phil Harding doing what he does best: flint knapping. He first had to make the basic flint tool for the programme's cameo. This was a boring tool called a 'burin', a flint blade that has had a piece removed to create a ninety degree angle. With this

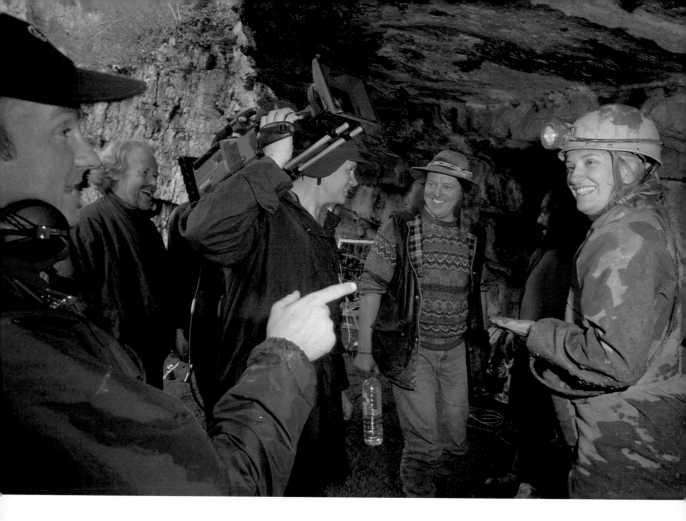

Previous page: Carenza, ten metres (thirty feet) down and at last in possession of what might be a crucial piece of evidence. The involvement of the crews in the emotion of the programme is something special to Time Team.

Above: Relief and excitement at the cave mouth after Andy Currant identified the bone as prehistoric. Carenza shares the moment with our regular soundman Steve Bowden.

he would make a *bâton de commandement*, one of the Upper Palaeolithic period's most enigmatic objects. Two examples had been found at nearby Gough's Cave. The term describes an object made from antler horn, often with a hole pierced in its thicker end. Like all such artefacts the *bâton* provides an ideal opportunity for academics to theorize. Suggestions as to its use include that it was a lasso and that its handle was used to gain extra purchase; that it helped climbers to ascend and provided a brake when they descended; that it was a thong-stropper to remove bits of flesh from leather thongs; an arrow straightener and, most interestingly, a sex aid. (The last explanation was suggested by my namesake Timothy Taylor, who has written an intriguing book on the sexual element in archaeological finds. The fact that we have the same name has often caused confusion. People come up to me and say with interest, 'So you are Timothy Taylor' – to which I have to reply, to their obvious disappointment, in the negative.) It seemed clear that making the object would be fairly straightforward for

Phil but that, given this wide interpretation, demonstrating its use might present problems.

On Day Three we began to get deeper in Trench 3 in the left-hand corner of the cave where a tunnel had been widened by cavers, but blocked off by a subsequent rock fall. It was another important area for us because, once again in the right-hand tunnel the Stal had been penetrated in the past. Carenza in her full caving kit committed herself to going deep into the cave interior to see if anything could be found. With Trench 1 in the car park now closed down and Trench 2 rapidly filling with mud and water, Trench 3 became our last chance. In the early part of the day small pieces of bone had been seen here and Carenza had clearly located an area where cave deposits had accumulated. With all the mud and silt around, it was difficult to see whether it was under the stal or just close to it. As time ran out she finally located one piece of bone with cut marks on it. Andy Currant, to everyone's delight, confirmed they had been made by a flint tool.

Conclusion

In his final report Andy Currant wrote that the bones from Trench 3 tied in well with the material which had just turned up in the zoology department of the Natural History Museum, claimed to be from Parry's dig in the 1930s, but that he did not see anything which couldn't be Iron Age – sadly including Carenza's fragment with cut marks. All the butchery marks he could find on the Cooper's Hole material at the museum were also made with stone tools. He concluded: 'The long and short of it is that we didn't really get far enough below the stalagmite floor to stand much of a chance of finding anything convincingly Upper Palaeolithic, but given the restrictions we were working under I suppose that was inevitable. I still find it very strange that archaeologists should go to such lengths to prevent us from finding any archaeology.'

I would hope this still allows us to suggest that our bones may have been Upper Palaeolithic – we just can't prove it.

Below: What all the fuss was about – you can just make out the scratches created by a stone tool.

Following page: One of the cavers, myself, Simon Raikes and Mick Worthington with what one of our researchers called 'the remains of a prehistoric Kentucky Fried Chicken dinner'.

CHAPTER 2

Burslem, Stoke-on-Trent

TONY'S PIECE TO CAMERA: 'Everyone knows the name of Wedgwood when it comes to pottery, and this is what they have in mind: the blue and white design which is famous throughout the world. But few people know that it was here in Burslem, on the outskirts of Stoke-on-Trent, that Josiah Wedgwood's climb to fame and fortune first began. This is actually the site of his first factory, which was at the heart of the pottery industry as it took off in the eighteenth century. But does any of it survive under the paving stones of modern-day Burslem?'

Above: *Local archaeologist, Bill Klemperer, shows Mick and Tony an engraving of buildings from the time of Wedgwood's first pottery.*

Opposite: *Fragments of nineteenth-century pottery – just the tip of the iceberg of our cache.*

Above: *The interior of a kiln – plus stationary exhibit – shows the complex brickwork needed to create the roof structure.*

Burslem was originally billed as the dig that would unearth Josiah Wedgwood's first kiln. The site was suggested by Bill Klemperer, Stoke-on-Trent's city archaeologist, and pursued with some tenacity by researcher Julian Hudson. Wedgwood's role as one of the key figures of the Industrial Revolution made his Ivy House Works a tempting target. However, it had been occupied by kilns for decades after his departure and its location in the centre of Burslem, now a part of Stoke-on-Trent, meant that I needed some convincing before we went ahead.

Urban archaeology has produced fascinating sites for the *Time Team* in the past, but they have been accompanied by the difficulties of digging in close proximity to a jumble of concrete, pipes and cables. I still have clear memories of some of the trenches we dug on the site of Matthew Boulton's mint in Birmingham in Series 4, where deep, unstable trenches were filled with brick rubble, piping for utility services and a large underground petrol tank that leaked fumes. The Wedgwood site raised some difficult questions. Would the substantial later buildings, including the neo-classical meat market, have buried or destroyed the site? Would we be able to tell the difference between an early Wedgwood kiln and the layers of later kilns? The deeper the researchers went, and the more information we began to accumulate, the more the site began to appeal to me.

We were dealing with a relatively narrow period of time. Wedgwood had occupied the site for less than four years, from 1759 to 1762. He had early declared, in a manner characteristic of the time, that he wanted to be 'pottery maker to the universe' and there were many similarities between him and Matthew Boulton. Both men were at the forefront of the Industrial Revolution. In their respective fields they developed methods of production that saw a massive increase in the output of two of our most basic objects: coins and household pottery. The transition from individual artisans creating unique artefacts that could often be traced to their particular style had been replaced by a world where mass production created thousands of identical objects in an unbelievably short time.

Wedgwood's desire to put decent, highly glazed pottery into every home was mirrored by Boulton's wish to provide everyone with coins that could not be counterfeited and were worth their face value. They both combined rigorous and energetic entrepreneurial skills with a social conscience, and saw the whole world as their potential market.

As with Boulton's factory, a plan of the Burslem site which would help us to locate individual buildings on the ground was a key piece of information. In more recent times it had been covered by a car park and a small square with trees, lawns and flowerbeds, plus seats and a bandstand. The area had been selected as the location of Ceramica, a community-based project, funded partly by the Millennium Commission, to restore Burslem's old town hall and the surrounding square and create a new pottery museum and heritage centre that would celebrate the history of the potteries. The project, initiated by local people, started in 1995 and it is expected that the museum, which will take into account the archaeology we found over the three days, will be completed and open to the public in 1999.

We knew that at an early stage in the filming it would be useful to show the archaeologists the kind of pottery to look out for, and a group of local experts selected some key pieces and placed them in chronological order. The imaginative designs with their different colours and shapes were an introduction to the variety of material we hoped to find.

The great virtue of pottery to the archaeologist is that it continually changes in style and that these changes can be dated. A series of pieces of pots or other artefacts, such as brooches or swords that can be placed in historical order, is called a typology. Each object has its date and therefore serves as a frame of reference for similar ones found at other sites. For us, one of the key types of pottery would be Wedgwood's creamware. We know from documentary records that it was produced at a certain date, and if it turned up underneath a layer of bricks we would know that the bricks had been laid after the last date for the first production of this style of pottery. Large amounts of creamware associated with one layer would be strong dating evidence. However, layers in a trench can be confusing.

The critical judgement is always whether or not we can be sure that an object comes from a particular layer, or has worked its way up or down from adjacent ones. In the trenches at Stoke-on-Trent there were layers of eighteenth-century buildings with nineteenth-century features cutting into them. Excavation in these circumstances has to be highly skilful to get an idea of the relative order of the material you are finding.

Mick often uses the analogy of eating a trifle to explain the point. If you dive straight into it and drag out the nice bits at the bottom – the archaeological equivalent of the pieces of sherry-soaked sponge –

Above: Creamware: the key artefact linking our excavation back to Wedgwood pottery.

Team Profile

Julian Hudson – *Researcher*

'I loved Wedgwood because of the sense of community that surrounded the shoot and the ease with which it seemed to work. I felt it was a job well done in true archaeological fashion.

'I was drawn to the aspect of 'how' we knew what we knew about the past at school, so after leaving I joined a local archaeology company as a volunteer digger and a year later went on to do a degree in archaeology. My first professional experience was as a site supervisor, followed by contractor after completing an MA in Archaeological Survey. In that time I went to Jerusalem for six weeks to do a 'Medieval and Ottoman Survey Project', which was tremendously exciting and allowed us privileged access to areas of the city.

'Getting into television from there was really a stroke of luck. I had been fascinated by the idea of working in the media for a while and made contact with an old friend who was working on a programme about dinosaurs for the Discovery Channel. Consequently I was taken on for five weeks' work experience in April 1996 and I left two years later to join *Time Team*, having become a researcher.'

Opposite: A visit to a complete kiln for comparison with the remains we were finding. As is often the case on Time Team, *the camera is hand held.*

everything gets mixed up. In an excavation, if you remove every layer carefully you stand a chance of working out what comes from each one and the order or chronology of the site. People who dig holes in pursuit of objects risk losing track of the layers or, to give them their archaeological label, contexts, and may remove the one critical artefact that would have dated a lower layer. It is a fairly regular occurrence that later activity on a site cuts through earlier contexts. For instance, on *Time Team* we have come across Roman sites with Anglo-Saxon pits dug into them. This perhaps helps to explain why archaeology can be so confusing – and, as Mick says, why it is always interesting to see how an archaeologist eats a trifle!

The particular trifle we were dealing with in Burslem soon duly produced some confused and interesting layers, and in Trench 1 we hit

Above: Mick overlooks the site of Trench 1 where the JCB is well underway. The noisy traffic presented major challenges to our sound crew.

the solid remains of the meat market which had been built in 1835 and demolished in 1957. A brick building with a stone façade, it had been twice the size of the adjacent town hall.

A large area of concrete sealed the surface and we needed heavy equipment to dig below it. Anyone who has hit concrete with a pickaxe will know that it is one of the construction industry's more unpleasant and solid inventions. A mechanical digger equipped with a concrete-breaker was necessary and we were lucky to have an expert to operate it. Kevin Grainger, a demonstration driver for JCB in Rochester, was on hand for the three days with a 3CX Backhoe loader.

I have watched skilled digger-drivers in action on many of our sites and seen how they arouse mixed emotions in archaeologists. However, to remove large amounts of sterile topsoil or urban rubble by hand is a waste of everyone's time and energy, and many sites would not be excavated if the work was restricted to hand digging. A good digger-driver can remove thin layers with great care and, with an expert holding a watching brief, most archaeologists would accept that this is perfectly sensible practice.

John and Chris had brought ground-penetrating radar which was needed to get through the tarmac covering the car-park site. This is being used ever more frequently in archaeology because it can provide detailed information about the depth and form of deposits. An electromagnetic field is transmitted into the ground and reflected back to the surface by buried features such as ditches, walls, etc. so that a series of vertical and horizontal slices through the ground can be viewed. He managed to get a response that could be the northern extension of the Ivy Works although we knew that a police station and air-raid shelter had been built in the area at a later date, after the pottery. A trench here became Trench 4.

Time Team has had mixed results with radar. In the early days a number of different companies tried to sell it as the answer to all archaeologists' prayers, almost as though there would be no need to dig any more. However, the reality was that we ended up with yards of attractive colour print-outs that never seemed to quite locate what had been expected. The reasons for this were bafflingly scientific. Added to

Below: *Heavy plant machinery in action. Urban archaeology can require severe measures.*

Above: Meeting the local diggers for a cup of tea before we start. We give them an outline of what we hope to achieve while thay give us useful background on the site.

Opposite: The director, Graham Dixon, holds a lightweight monitor and the soon-to-be-amended script. He keeps in contact with crew members via a microphone and earpiece.

the problem of failure to locate was the fact that you need a three-dimensional imagination to interpret the slices that radar produces. With resistance surveys or magnetometry you see the target in plan – that is, with good results the shape of a building emerges as though seen from above. In the last year our radar results have been more positive, possibly because our resident geophysics team have been operating the latest gear and have a better idea of how their findings need to be shown on screen. Geophysics results and landscape surveys all require processing time and the delay in getting an answer has to be built into the programme's schedule. I am endlessly asking John or Chris for an estimated time of arrival for the latest print-out. They in turn have to face the difficulties of operating computer gear in the field.

One of the big differences between *Time Team* excavations and many others that use geophysics is that we start digging relatively soon after the results have been interpreted. There is no delayed gratification. On conventional sites it is often years before trenches are dug which means that the geophysics team have to wait to calibrate their readings against the reality of what they see, before they can confirm the nature of similar readings elsewhere on the site.

By the end of Day One two trenches were open. Trench 1, the one nearest the road, revealed a rather nice Victorian tiled floor. In Trench 2, near the bandstand, there was an area of bricks that seemed to be made up of a number of layers. This was the first possible indication of a kiln but there was no pottery and no other dating evidence. The lower layer of brick looked much older than the one above. It was made of clay that seemed to contain a number of different-coloured elements as opposed to the more uniform body of the later bricks. There was also a structure that appeared to be a drain but might be part of the kiln cutting into the excavation. Interpreting this jumble of layers looked daunting, and the solid nature of the upper foundations made me concerned that the later building might have wiped out the earlier evidence we were looking for.

As usual our discoveries were beginning to conflict with the script – the key bit of paper with which we head into a *Time Team* programme – and Graham Dixon, the director, had to adjust to the reality of the finds in Trench 1 and Trench 2.

The likely route of the next day's archaeology has to be reflected in the schedule, which tells everyone what will be shot when. *Time Team* often works with three camera crews which can mean that a number of critical scenes are shot at the same time. In this case the director takes the main area, which usually involves Tony, and the associate producers and researchers are briefed to look after the other crews. I move between the three trying to judge where the archaeology is heading and when we need to change our plans to meet the next archaeological twist of fate. At Burslem we decided to concentrate more of our time on the material coming from Trench 2.

The other bit of paper that is often useful is an improvised plan of the site that shows the location of the trenches as they go in. Letting viewers know exactly where they are in relation to each one is always a concern and a site with several trenches can be confusing. The plan frequently makes an appearance on screen and we always try to have paper and large felt tip pens handy to allow Mick or Tony to sketch out the geography for the viewer. The crane shot, which gives an overhead view of the site, and which we have used increasingly in recent series, is also helpful.

Opposite: *On top of an increasingly large pile of pottery, I take five minutes to check where we are in the script and if it is matching the reality of the trenches. The sodden condition of the script was the result of a spectacular downpour.*

Above: *The glimpse of brickwork that gave us the first clue that we might be on top of an early kiln.*

Day Two saw the dig extending further into the square and coming dangerously close to the flowerbeds. Trench 3 required benches to be removed and large paving slabs, virtually on the steps of the town hall, to be pulled up. By now news of our presence had spread and hundreds of spectators had arrived, including members of what appeared to be a Phil Harding fan club. *Time Team* excavations have always been as open as possible within the constraints of health and safety issues. We are unearthing the history and archaeology of the local community and we try to show people what is going on. In this case we had to erect a wire fence because the trenches were unstable and there were so many visitors. We had foreseen this and the council proved helpful in providing the fencing. Our security guards, who give me a sense of comfort on all dangerous sites, were also on hand. They not only keep an eye on members of the public and prevent them, in a friendly way, from getting too near dangerous bits of the dig, but also protect the gear overnight. During a recent programme the night shift had been alert enough to realize that some characters who turned up with a low loader and said they had come to collect our mechanical digger were in fact attempting to steal it. By and large, because we do

Opposite: John Gater, Carenza and Bernard Thomason check the geophysics results against earlier plans to see if they match up. This is a critical stage in judging where to put trenches.

Below: Trench 3, adjacent to the old town hall and some flower beds, was to produce a vast amount of pottery.

CHAPTER 3

Beauport Park, Sussex

TONY'S PIECE TO CAMERA: 'This is the thirteenth fairway of a golf course in East Sussex, but just over there in the woods, a Roman bath house has been discovered. It's an incredible find, complete with underfloor heating, tiled floors, and walls which survive up to window height. But what is a Roman bath house doing here completely on its own, forty miles from the nearest Roman town? What was happening here 1,900 years ago?'

Opposite: Jake Keen begins our attempt to reproduce a furnace for melting iron. Local clay and straw are being compressed. Later they will be dried out by a slow-burning fire.

Above: Somewhere in the woods, under a camouflage of tin roofs and plastic, was a unique archaeological site from the Roman period.

The Romans in Britain

The army of the Roman Empire first set foot on British soil in 55 BC, led by Julius Caesar, but failed to gain a permanent foothold. This was left to the emperor Claudius who invaded Britain successfully in AD 43. His invasion force was said to have included a couple of elephants and I have always wondered whether their graves might be awaiting a *Time Team* dig somewhere in the south-east ... or did Claudius take them back?

Britain had an attractive set of natural resources for the Romans to exploit – iron, tin, gold and lead in abundance – and they mined these from the earliest days of occupation. Not surprisingly, the British were not delighted to be under the Roman yoke and most mining operations came under the command of the military. In one of the earliest *Time Team* programmes, at Rochester in Kent, we saw a reconstruction of a defensive ditch built by Roman legionaries. It was an effective demonstration of how civil engineering at the edges of the empire had to be undertaken by men who could defend themselves if necessary.

The Romans needed ironwork for swords, shield bosses and a wide range of military equipment. They also used iron farming implements and fittings in houses. There is some evidence that so much iron was made in the Weald that it was exported overseas. The baths at Beauport Park were found under a massive pile of iron slag, which had clearly come from a major ironworking site.

Bath houses are fascinating structures and symbolize the Romans' desire for civilised facilities even in this far-flung edge of the Empire. They were part of the social life of the Roman Empire, not just places for getting clean in, and bathing involved an elaborate ritual. When a Roman official retired to one of them he put his clothes in a 'locker' in the changing room, the *apodyterium*, near the entrance, and plunged into a cold pool in a room called the *frigidarium*. He then moved on to a warm pool in the *tepidarium* and, finally, a hot one in the *caldarium*. Here his body was oiled, often by slaves, and his skin was scraped with a *strigil* – a blunt blade that removed oil and dirt. There was often an exercise area and a place where bathers could relax after a final plunge in the cold pool.

To exist at all, bath houses needed sophisticated building techniques and efficient channelling of natural resources. A complex system of plumbing distributed warm and hot water to the pools in the *tepidarium* and *caldarium*. The rooms themselves were kept at the required temperatures by furnaces that sent hot air through a series of hollow pipes under the floors and in the walls – without releasing deadly waste gases. The Romans developed waterproof cement, *opus signinum*, for the floors. These were suspended and often decorated with mosaics, which required vast numbers of tiles and skilled builders to lay them. The box-flue tiles with their distinctive scored surfaces that provided a key for plaster are one of the most easily recognizable clues to the existence of a bath house. In the case of the Beauport Park site a number of roof tiles had been found stamped with the letters CL-BR. This identifies them as belonging to the imperial fleet in Britain, the *classis Britannica*, the seaborne wing of the Roman army whose officers were also in charge of iron production.

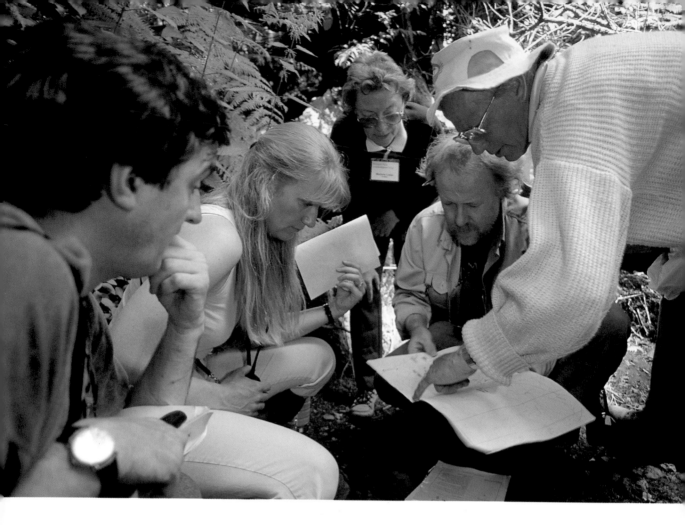

Above: *Local amateur archaeologists point to the areas of previous excavations while Guy de la Bédoyère, Carenza and I try to make sense of it all.*

At Beauport Park near Battle in Sussex we were dealing with one of the best preserved, standing Roman buildings in southern England. Walls up to 2.4 metres (eight feet) high with window ledges make it a unique site. It also has 'lockers' where bathers kept their clothes. These have been found intact in only a few other sites in Europe – the bath house at Chesters (the Roman Cilurnum), on Hadrian's Wall, Pompeii, Herculaneum and two sites in Spain. They have also been found in Herod's bath house at Masada in Israel.

Although the site is close to the Beauport Park golf club the owners of the club were interested and helpful, and took the view that archaeology might attract tourists. However, we agreed not to dig up the golf course if this could be avoided. The site is surrounded by woodland and a small stream runs through it. Scheduling would restrict us to an area outside the main bath house area.

The bath house was found by Dr Gerald Bodribb, an amateur archaeologist. Guy de la Bédoyère, our Roman expert whose book

Roman Villas and the Countryside had proved invaluable on the live shoot at Turkdean in Gloucestershire in 1997, had contacted us about the site. One of the key ideas he wanted to test was the theory that the bath house did not stand alone and that there would be other buildings such as houses occupied by officers. These officers would have been in charge of the ironworks which would have produced the iron slag under which the bath house had been buried, and it would have been built for them. As Guy said in his initial research document, Britain's natural resources – such as iron – were the property of the Roman emperor and their care would therefore have been the responsibility of high-ranking officials. At an early stage I had wondered whether the baths could have been the equivalent of pithead showers in a coalfield, but he was adamant that only senior officers would have used them, and that most workers would have been little better than slaves.

Guy alerted us to the fact that in Roman times the coastline would have been closer to Beauport Park than it is now, which would have made exporting the finished iron easier than it seems today. This partly helps to explain the anomaly that the bath house is miles from any Roman town or fort.

He also supplied details about the possible name of an officer connected with the bath house. Guy pointed out that an altar at the Roman-Saxon shore fort of Lympne in Kent had been erected by a commander of the fleet, Lucius Aufidius Pantera. By a bit of clever research into other fleet commanders connected with him, Guy had chanced upon Quintus Baienus Blassianus whose name bears a striking similarity to the one recorded on an inscription found at the ironworks: Bassianus. This is the kind of information that unfortunately never makes it into the final programme but is nevertheless fascinating. By and large, *Time Team* is about the results of an excavation – it is not a history programme – but we give the general historical background to set a site in its context.

Henry Cleere, an ex-director of the Council for British Archaeology and one of the experts who worked on the site, believed that the ironworks might be one of the biggest in the Roman Empire. He estimated that it could have yielded more than 200 tons of iron each year – as much as forty per cent of the total produced in Britain. This would have required fifty tons of charcoal a day, destroying massive numbers of hardwood trees in the locality. The large areas of deciduous woodland, including hardwoods like oak, that surround the site today are just a reminder of the vast forests that once covered the region.

In order to understand exactly the nature of what we would be looking for, an understanding of how iron was made would be important. Iron production was in many ways the final stage of a series of metallurgical developments that started with copper and bronze and enabled cultures to use the natural resources that were available to them. Although iron is more common than copper it is harder to extract because it requires a higher temperature. By the Roman period there was a vast requirement for iron which was used for weapons, domestic tools, buildings (nails and cramps) and the whole range of fittings that held boats together.

Iron had not always been acquired by smelting: earlier cultures and native American and Inuit tribes obtained it from meteorites and saw it as a metal from heaven. However, in many areas it is combined with oxygen as an oxide. Magnetite, limonite and haematite are the main forms, some of which can be used as red dyes. Combined with other minerals as ores they require temperatures somewhere in the region of 1,300°C (2,372°F) and the presence of carbon for the iron to be extracted. The ore is mixed with charcoal and as the temperature in the furnace rises the oxygen and other impurities separate out from the ore to form slag. The iron, still with some other materials, forms a bloom at the base of the furnace. This is removed and hammered by a smith to extract the remaining impurities. Slag looks metallic but is largely made of a non-magnetic substance called fairlight. This is one of the main by-products of an ironworks and was useful for building roads because it is easily compacted and drains well.

Iron was used in the Middle East as early as 3,000 BC but in central Europe ironworking is associated with the Hallstatt period of the Early Iron Age (c.800–c.500 BC) and the earliest known examples of iron-smelting furnaces come from Austria at the end of that era. Once the technological problems of extracting iron from ore had been solved it became more easily available and many cultures were able to take advantage of it. Some historians refer to iron as the 'democratic' metal. As smiths began to learn the secrets of the new material, they found that welding sheets of iron that had different degrees of hardness could produce a durable sharp edge. Because iron is worked in the presence of carbon it begins to absorb it and this starts the process that creates the harder metal we call steel.

Dr Gerald Bodribb has spent a large part of his life uncovering the secrets of the site he discovered and it was clear that anything we could do to support him would be worthwhile. When we first saw the bath house it was in a state of suspended archaeological animation. The walls were protected with plastic bags and the site was covered by a tin roof.

We had come across a bath house, or at least the remains of a plunge pool, at Turkdean. I had by now become cautious about the chances of finding a mosaic. At Turkdean we had uncovered a large villa but no mosaic.

Throughout Britain there are Roman sites of great importance that now lie hidden under sand, which is the standard way of backfilling and protecting excavated buildings. The Beauport Park bath house is in many ways an illustration of why this happens, and why English Heritage and other archaeological bodies are so cautious about uncovering additional sites. The reasons are fairly clear. Inevitably, they can begin to deteriorate when they are uncovered. Weather and the attention of vandals can soon begin to damage unique archaeology and the bill to stabilize and protect a site can be huge. It would be almost

Team Profile

Katy Hirst – *Digger*

'My first practical experience of archaeology was at the age of eighteen when my father, who was working in the Middle East, managed to get me on to a site in Oman that was being excavated by Italian archaeologists. I went on to do a degree in archaeology at Durham University and have been a professional archaeologist since 1992. My most exciting find was a Bronze Age necklace with a gold pendant that I found on a child skeleton in Syria. The period I most enjoy studying is prehistory, in particular the rituals.

'The job can be quite strenuous, particularly on *Time Team* when you need to complete a lot of work in a short space of time, which piles on the pressure. I first worked on the series when they were looking for diggers while on a shoot in Carlisle. They contacted the Carlisle unit where I work and I leapt at the opportunity, much to the envy of my fellow archaeologists. Of the *Time Team* digs I have been on, I particularly enjoyed the Roman site at Papcastle because of the rich source of finds that we uncovered.

'I would urge anyone considering archaeology as a career to think very carefully, because it is not a profession that will make you rich. If it seems desirable despite this, I would suggest taking a university course because it is very difficult to get into it through straight digging. For myself, the process of uncovering something amazing that has been hidden for hundreds, even thousands, of years is tremendously rewarding.'

impossible to meet the projected cost without a favourable lottery bid. The English Heritage's response to knowing about an important but buried Roman site is often that it is best to leave it until they can find some way of protecting it and meeting the bill for its care. One of the largest mosaics in southern Britain is buried in Woodchester in Wiltshire, but it will probably never be seen by our generation because

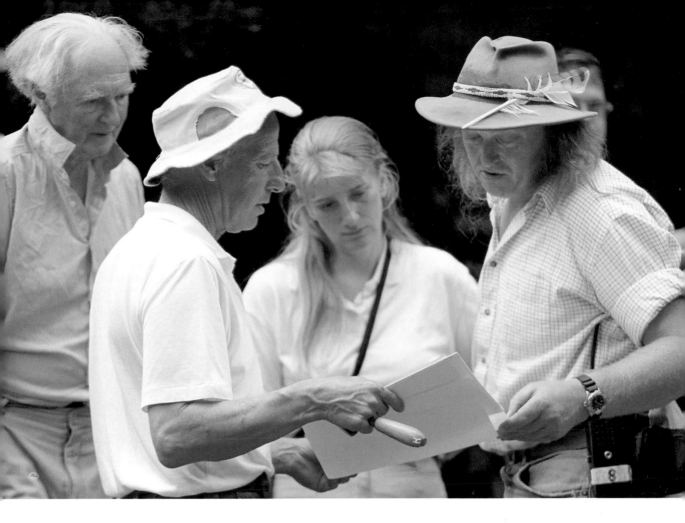

there are no funds to display and protect it. The irony is, of course, that until a site is exposed it is impossible to tell what condition it is in, and therefore whether it is worth pursuing and what the likely costs will be.

Gerald had gathered a group of enthusiastic helpers around him, some of whom claimed that they could use divining rods to locate archaeology. They had toiled around the bath-house site attempting to trace other areas of Roman activity. Without any funds their work had always been voluntary. They were dependent on their own devices and without the benefit of advice from professional architects had often not recorded opened-up areas and small trial digs accurately. In some cases it seemed that digs had been cut through the archaeology in order to pursue a particular find.

Inevitably, there was a lack of adequate plans and careful mapping of finds, and no section drawings showing the sides of trenches and recording the various layers and where finds were located. Any archaeological judgement of Beauport Park would be hampered

Above: Gerald Bodribb, who found the bath house, looks on as a local archaeologist shows Phil and Carenza records from the previous digs.

because in many cases all we knew was that Roman pottery and other artefacts had come from various holes scattered throughout the site. There was plenty of evidence of activity, but without consistent records of the exact distribution, location, depth and quality of the material it was difficult to decide where the key areas were located.

On the first day I was given a guided tour of the site, particularly the area hidden under the woods bordering the small stream that runs through it. As we staggered through the nettles and waist-high weeds various diggings were pointed out to me. There seemed to be rather a lot of them and as the cartoon shows it reminded us of gruyère cheese.

Guy and Gerald had discussed possible targets in the areas surrounding the site with us. An initial survey by Gerald and his team had located platforms that might be the possible site of buildings, and these were the areas we decided to concentrate on initially. They would be the location for our first three trenches. They were about 110 metres (366 feet) from the bath house and each one was just large enough –

about ninety square metres (270 square feet) – to encompass a building. There were two obstacles to excavating them: thick undergrowth and the fact that the site was surrounded by the green fairways of the golf course. The first day's events took on a rather surreal quality as we excavated alongside the golfers' paths with the odd ball sailing over our heads.

Each site required a major effort to clear the bracken and brushwood so that the geophysics team could do its survey. The initial results were disappointing and as we began to cast our net further afield I looked again at the bath house site, and wondered whether we should be dealing with a much smaller area immediately to its north-west. A large area here had been scheduled but within it there were open excavations that had not, as far as we could tell, been drawn or recorded. At this stage I thought it might be useful if we recorded them. However, we first had to obtain permission to work in the scheduled area.

The local English Heritage inspector, Peter Kendall, took the view that recording the existing excavations more accurately and providing drawings of the section would be a valuable piece of work in terms of understanding the site, and sanctioned a limited exercise to record it. I agreed with him that before we proceeded we would check with Andy Woodcock, the county archaeologist, who had agreed to act as our archaeological policeman. He proved to be a tremendous help.

Jenni Butterworth was sent into the woods to record the open digs and first had to clear the vegetation. Only one small excavation within the scheduled area could be easily accessed, where Roman pottery had been located but no section drawings had been done.

By the end of Day One we had drawn a blank with the first platform site even though we had put three trenches in there, and had to expand our area. Jenni had had some success in extracting slag from the hole left by a fallen tree which we were calling Trench 4. But we still didn't have any buildings. We were working on the idea that the high ground surrounding the ironworkings was a likely location for a villa. Mick and I strolled away from the excavation and filming in order to explore some of these areas.

Following page: *On the thirteenth fairway the archaeologists and golfers come into close proximity. Stewart Ainsworth and Mick are working out where the areas of high ground might be while a researcher checks the likely trajectory of the next ball.*

Beauport Park, Sussex   101

Team Profile

Jenni Butterworth – *Digger*

'I was always interested in history as a child, and found archaeology a more interesting version of the subject. I began as a volunteer in a museum ten years ago while still at school, and decided to study archaeology at Bristol University where I met Mick Aston. He is passionate about medieval archaeology, particularly monasteries. This also appealed to me so I started studying with him for a PhD, which I am still in the process of finishing. I think Mick is a humorous speaker, with a great talent for presenting a lot of information in a way that makes it seem interesting and easy to understand.

During my career as an archaeologist I have had many direct experiences with the past, most profoundly when we dug up a piece of timber on the Somerset Levels for *Time Team*. When it was dendro-dated it was found to have been felled in about 900 BC. After we pulled it out you could still see all the tool marks where the man had cut the timber before it had been put in the ground.

My most exciting dig on *Time Team*, though, would have to be Beauport Park in Battle, because even though the finds were not numerous it proved that by working archaeologically you can still piece a story together.

'I enjoyed the Stoke-on-Trent dig very much because I love pottery and we found tons of it. We weren't sure whether there would be anything left of Wedgwood's factory, and the site didn't look very promising, so when the first shards began to appear it was tremendously exciting. Then there was more and more and more... I think the local archaeologists were used to recovering so many finds, but for *Time Team* it was a truly astonishing experience.

'Archaeology can be hard work and difficult at times, particularly when it starts to rain and you are trying to draw records of the trench. What is exciting and keeps you motivated is the variety in the job, and the combination of physical labour and intellect. Being an archaeologist and looking at the past makes things around you – the landscape and living environments – more understandable. You can look at them with new eyes and understand why things are the way they are.

'I am often asked if I think archaeology is a predominantly male career and the answer is, not any more. More and more women are getting involved. In the past it may have been dominated by men because of the predominantly male academic community and the job's very physical nature.

In the woodland we hacked our way through the undergrowth looking for signs of earthworks. It is a fairly common occurrence that at some point during a *Time Team* dig Mick and I will take time to assess what's going on, usually when one or other of us says, 'I need to have a chat.' We both know that this is a chance to think about where we are going and, if necessary, take a new angle on our strategy. These conversations are always important and I stop the filming if Mick feels we are heading in the wrong direction.

The schedule directors used to push the story forward, and the relative lack of time to achieve our stated goals, can provide pressure to pursue one set course of action. I have always made it clear to Mick that if he is not comfortable with the direction in which we are heading I will stop the process and reassess our objectives. If I am concerned about a reality that we seem to be ignoring I share it with him and then warn the director of a likely change of tack. A major part of my job is to keep an eye on the archaeology and to pass likely developments on to the director. At Burslem, in this series, I had been able to alert him to the

Below: Jenni Butterworth with a piece of Roman glass. The design would have been created by blowing glass into a mould.

now opened Trench 8 on a geophysical anomaly at the side of the thirteenth fairway.

The presence of ironworkings gave us the chance to attempt the reconstruction of an iron-smelting furnace as the cameo. This was a major undertaking. We called on the services of Jake Keen, who had helped us out before on *Time Team*, and Gerry McDonnell, an archaeo-metallurgist from Bradford. Gerry had been involved in one of the very first *Time Team* programmes when we had been excavating the site of Alfred's abbey at Wedmore in Somerset. A piece of an iron bloom, the lump of metal that is left in a furnace after smelting, had appeared during a field walk around the abbey and after a telephone call from Chris, Gerry had dropped everything to head down the motorway to identify it. What was fascinating was to listen to his description of the bits and pieces of ironworking debris that lay around the site. He could judge the quality of the furnace by the nature of the slag. As we walked through the woods on an initial recce he would pick up pieces and say, 'Yes, this is excellent stuff.' Good slag means the temperature in the furnace was high enough to remove many of the impurities.

The choice of cameo was easy but carrying it out was a different matter. We had reproduced glass at a Roman site at Lavenham in Suffolk, in Cornwall we had smelted tin and at Papcastle in Cumbria we had fired pottery, but ironworking is tricky. Aside from the temperature of over 1,300°C (2,372°F) that it requires, a complete absence of oxygen is essential at a critical point in the smelting process. Ella Galinski, our assistant producer, trawled through our usual contacts and met with a general air of doubt and scepticism: all the experts said it would

OH, I SAY! A HOLE IN ONE!

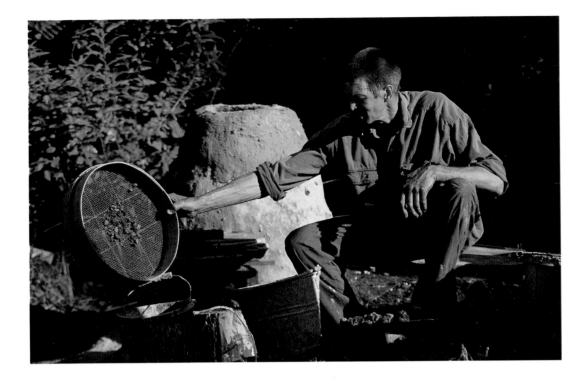

be impossible to reconstruct a furnace and fire within three days. The clay would have to dry out slowly, and it would be necessary to warm up the furnace gradually or it would crack and allow oxygen to enter. This meant a week to build the furnace and a couple of days to get it up to the right temperature for smelting.

Jake Keen was an ideal 'cameo' expert, willing to try and perhaps fail. His reaction was that it could be done in three days – with the right kind of clay. This was obtained from a local quarry. He approached the task of building the furnace with great energy, accompanied by Reg Miles who assisted him and would be on hand to form the iron from the kiln. We had located an area of ore near the site, probably the remains of the material the Romans had used, and Phil helped to collect this. He is our key *Time Team* person when it comes to reconstructions, and is always enthusiastic about learning a new skill.

We knew that the keys to success would be the quality of the furnace construction and achieving a fire that was hot enough to allow reduction – when oxygen is extracted from the ore and the impurities drain off to leave pure iron behind – to take place. By setting a series of gentle fires within the furnace, Jake managed to dry it out more quickly

Above: Jake Keen with his precious sample of ore and the furnace waiting to be fired – a scene not dissimilar to one from Roman times.

than the experts had predicted. I was surprised at how small it was: I had imagined a large structure but this looked like an oversized beehive. Once it was dry, ore and locally produced charcoal were fed into it and a team of helpers manned bellows to keep the fire going. Gerry checked the heat level in the furnace with a temperature gauge, and at a critical point the furnace was closed off, reduction took place and the slag was tapped off.

Waiting for it to appear was an anxious time – and even when the volcanic-like substance dripped from the furnace we weren't sure whether there was anything left in the kiln. If there had been too many impurities in the ore there would be huge amounts of slag and no bloom. All went well, however, and the final act of extracting the iron and working it in raw form was a fascinating piece of reconstruction. To see material that had a day earlier been rock-like ore turned into a metal that glinted in the sun was a major *Time Team* achievement.

As we watched our group of reconstruction experts toiling in the heat we had some idea, for the first time, of what the site might have looked like during the Roman period. There would have been hundreds of these furnaces, and thousands of smiths working the hot iron into shape.

Opposite: *Jake Keen charging the furnace with ore and charcoal, a critical stage in the making of iron.*

Above: *A crucial moment. Tapping the slag tells us if the furnace has done its work. The crew braved the heat and smoke to get the best position to film Phil and Jake's spontaneous reaction.*

Following page: *The glowing evidence of success. Phil holds the spongy bit of iron that would become the end product of our three days' labour.*

Team Profile

Ella Galinski– *Associate Producer*

'I have been with *Time Team* since the beginning of the series and worked as assistant producer on the preceding *Time Signs* programmes, which was when I first became interested in archaeology.

'After gaining an MA in Drama and Theatre Arts, I moved into acting and, amongst other things, toured Europe with the Fragile Theatre Company, which was based in Italy. Later, having damaged my voice, I decided to concentrate on production and, after a brief spell as a set designer for an advertizing photographer, I joined Videotext who, at that time, were making educational videos. As in any small company I did everything from making sandwiches to writing, shooting and editing my own material.

'*Time Team* is such a people orientated production and I love trying to capture the spontaneous emotions on screen – the enthusiasm, excitement and disappointment as the narrative unfolds.

'The iron smelting experiment at Beauport Park was one of the most difficult and satisfying challenges. The atmosphere amongst the group of enthusiasts attempting the almost impossible within three days was quite electric and when the alchemy occurred the sense of achievement was thrilling. These cameos are often logistically tricky because you can rarely stop the action and shoot again – you have to capture everything as it happens. However, this makes for good television as it captures all the excitement as it evolves.'

Opposite: Hammering out the final piece of iron sent sparks flying and reproduced a skill that had last taken place on this site 1,700 years ago.

The lack of any buildings meant that we were now concentrating on evidence of ironworking. We had begun to get better geophysics results from areas nearer the main fairway. An earlier excavation had located a furnace and it seemed that Trench 9, the trench Jenni was clearing up, also contained the fired base of one. Each trench brought us nearer the edge of the golf course and we had to rely on the goodwill of

the owners to allow us to dig closer to the fairway – and the speed of the diggers' reactions to evade the golf balls. Trench 10 went into the edge of the rough on the thirteenth fairway.

On Day Three, Carenza and Phil spent some time working alongside members of the local group in Trench 11, an area that had been excavated previously. They were able to show the local archaeologists a standardized set of digging and recording methods that archaeologists use to understand the site. Trenches 12 and 13 followed on more earthworks. Our efforts began to have all the appearance of what my father calls a 'poke and hope' strategy, until Trench 13 found a furnace base and Trench 14, our last big geophysics target, located a charcoal-working pit. Charcoal is a key ingredient of ironworking because it allows a higher temperature to be reached in the furnace and there would have been a number of charcoal-burning sites in the area around the ironworks.

Below: With a quick rub from a file, Phil is able to catch the sunlight glinting on the surface of the finished product.

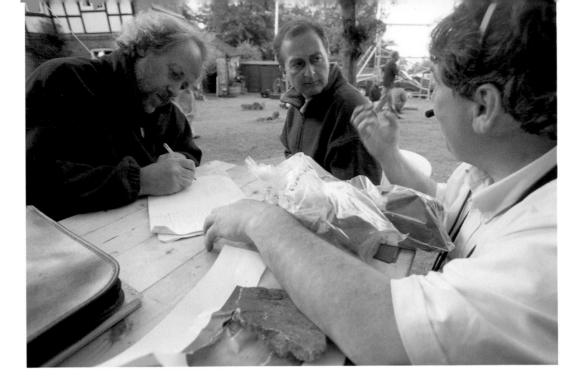

Conclusion

It now looks as if the fleet officers who managed the ironworks lived some distance away, perhaps by the coast, and only made passing visits to the site. There is a chance, however, that their accommodation lies under the piles of slag that surround the bath house. In the words of Guy de la Bédoyère, the programme showed that 'in practice the Roman world wasn't always quite as predictable as is sometimes thought… nothing in archaeology is certain, but theories need to be formed and tested for there to be any progress'. The lack of mosaics in the bath house possibly hinted at a low-status establishment suitable for the use of local workers.

Beauport Park is typical of many archaeological sites which would have remained undiscovered without the enthusiastic hard work of amateur archaeologists such as the ones on the *Time Team* dig and it is clear that groups like these need help. With county archaeology departments strapped for cash and manpower, and under pressure to dig up a site for a bypass or supermarket, it is often difficult to support them. When a site is as potentially important as Beauport Park the all too likely response is to stop any further work, schedule it to give it some legal protection and then cover it. Resources for archaeology are finite, and bodies such as English Heritage have to decide which sites should receive their limited cash and which ones will have to be left fallow.

Above: *After a tiring weekend the final piece of business needs to be thrashed out. What can Tony say we have achieved? Director Graham Dixon and I work out the possibilities. Tony will then turn this into his own style for the camera.*

Following page: *Despite the archaeological frustrations of the site, the success of the ironworking and intensive team effort gave us all a feeling of pleasure at the end of the three days.*

CHAPTER 4

Smallhythe, Kent

TONY'S PIECE TO CAMERA: 'You wouldn't think that these ordinary looking fields and this marshy old drainage ditch had anything to do with Britain's great sea-going heritage – for a start, I'm miles from the coast at a place called Smallhythe in Kent. But around the time of the battle of Agincourt in the early 1400s, somewhere round here was a port and a royal shipyard big enough to build 1,000-ton battleships. But if that's true, where are they now? And where's the river or estuary where they launched great big wooden ships?'

Opposite: *This large trench with relatively few finds did eventually produce evidence of the silting that caused Smallhythe's demise.*

Above: *A 'delft' field. We would, by the end of Day Two, have placed a considerable number of trenches in this field.*

Medieval Shipbuilding

There is an enigma about medieval shipbuilding. We have good documentary records of the names of ships, the kings they were built for and, in some cases, paintings of these huge vessels with their flags proudly flying. Thanks to the excavation of wrecks like the *Mary Rose*, we also know what they would have contained. However, we know very little about the medieval dockyards in which they were built.

In the Middle Ages ships were among the primary weapons of war, built to carry battle into foreign realms. In times of peace they were often neglected and allowed to rot. This meant that the shipbuilding industry was always a source of irregular employment that was dependent on the whim of the king.

Smallhythe was at that time a port and the surrounding area, especially the Weald, would have provided the basic requirements for shipbuilding – iron ore for iron and woodland for timber. The 1,000 ton *Jesus* was built here, or nearby, in 1416 during the reign of Henry V (1413–22). He was also responsible for the 1,400 ton *Grace Dieu*. Remnants of this great ship still survive. Built in Southampton it was part of the fleet that carried Henry's army to France in the campaign that ended victoriously with the battle of Agincourt in 1415.

Henry VII (1485–1509) increased the British fleet with ships like the *Sovereign*

and the 1,000-ton *Regent*. The *Mary Fortune*, an eighty-oared barque, was built at Smallhythe in 1497. Ian Friel our medieval ship expert was able to tell us details about the *Mary Fortune*. Work began on 11 February and went on for sixteen weeks. The total cost of wages and material amounted to over £110 – more than nine years' wages for the skilled master shipwright in charge of the work. There were at least sixteen other shipwrights as well as sawyers, eight sailmakers, some labourers and a night-watchman. The ship consumed at least twenty-three tons of timber and more than 13,000 iron and wooden nails, along with many other items. The *Mary Fortune*'s five sails were sewn with 112 'sail needles' and the three-masted rig required eighty separate ropes. The basic timber and iron raw material probably all came from within a few miles of Smallhythe.

We believed that the edge of the Rother river which flowed past Smallhythe in the Middle Ages would have been an ideal site for a shipyard. However, on the first day of filming, as we stared at the flat landscape sixteen kilometres (ten miles) from the sea it was difficult to imagine magnificent boats being built here.

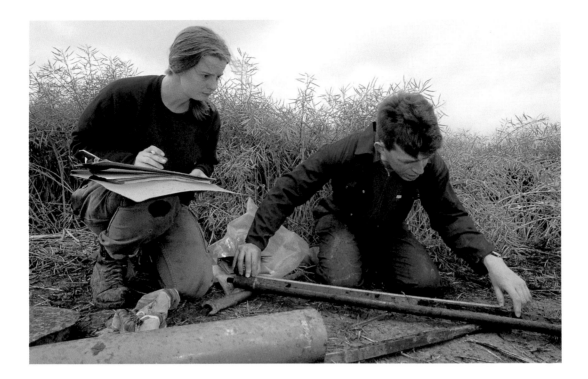

By Day Two we had little to show archaeologically for our efforts and John and Chris widened their search. However, we had started on the cameo, which was to become a really positive element in the programme. If you can't find a boat why not build one? The idea was to make a section of a ship from timber held together with iron nails and roves – the diamond-shaped washers that are placed over the ends of nails. This would be done by Andrew Baldwin, a smith, and Damian Goodburn who was a veteran of many *Time Team* reconstructions.

Damian and a team of carpenters had made a prehistoric log boat at Llangorse in Powys in Series 1 and the A-frame section of a medieval house for the Plympton, Devon, programme in Series 6. Even his best friends would admit that he is something of a slave-driver and a total perfectionist when he is engaged in his trade. He spares no one in his pursuit of the perfect wooden construction and regards the sappy green wood of freshly felled oak with almost religious fervour.

I have fond memories of the beautiful surface of the Llangorse boat, the wood newly felled and cut with a traditional adze. Constructing it had one of the essential requirements of a cameo: it was almost impossible to achieve. When we first contacted Damian about

Opposite: *John Gater giving the archaeology a good belt. The hammer blow creates the necessary vibration to begin recording seismic responses.*

Above: *Jane Siddell and Keith Wilkinson checking core samples. This gradually accumulated enough evidence to draw a profile of the area.*

Above: In the sandy layers of this trench we were able to see the gradual silting up that caused Smallhythe's demise. Jenni Butterworth's careful scraping illustrates the painstaking approach that is needed on trenches where the evidence is not obvious.

Opposite: An example of the language used in an archaeological report.

the reconstruction he said it would take a minimum of a month. We told him that he had three days but that he could have as many carpenters as he needed to help him – and he did it. Cameos that seem too easy always make me uncomfortable.

Reproducing the ship section at Smallhythe required hard work and skill but I did not feel that Damian had been pushed hard enough on Day One. However, by the end of Day Two cutting the nails and waterproofing the planks had injected the necessary air of excitement into the proceedings. Normally when ships' nails are used in large quantities a hole is drilled for each one where the planks overlap, the nail is pushed through and a diamond-shaped washer is placed over its tip on the inside of the boat. The tips are then cut off. Iron nails like the ones that were used in the Middle Ages are so hard that it is not feasible to use pincers.

For the cameo, Damian followed medieval practice and removed the tip of each nail by hitting it repeatedly and accurately with a small chisel-ended hammer – not without trepidation, because although he had researched this method by studying the tool marks on ships' nails that had been excavated in the London area it was the first time he had put his theory into practice. Also, our replica wrought-iron nails were a little harder than medieval ones would have been.

Peter Bellamy's Trench Report

'The stratigraphically earliest archaeological context was feature 507. It had vertical sides cut 0.3 m deep into the natural clay (505) and was roughly rectangular in plan, measuring 3.25 m by 2.70 m across, with an extension to the east at an angle of roughly 35 degrees. The eastern end was divided into two parts by a central pedestal of natural clay (502/503), though the complete arrangement of this end is not known as it had been partially destroyed by later activity. The sides and bottom of this feature were heavily burnt with extensive traces of vitrification. It was filled with a grey-brown silty clay (506), which contained a very large quantity of burnt clay fragments and occasional chalk flecks and patches of burnt chalk. Near the base of this layer was a large quantity of broken, vitrified bricks, with no apparent structure to them. At the eastern end there was a concentration of brick rubble around pedestal 502/503. These bricks were all handmade with both yellow and red fabrics present and occasional vitrified fragments.

The interpretation of this feature is hampered by the incomplete plan and the very small proportion of the feature which has been excavated. It appears to have been a clamp kiln of some sort with a rectangular kiln base and two angled flues at the eastern end.'

Smallhythe, Tenterden 1998

Plan

Trench 5

Plan labels: cut 507 · burnt natural · cut 507 · Kiln 507 · Slipway 508 · 506 · 502/ · bricks · 503 · 500 · 504 · bricks · burnt natural · cut 508 · 505

South-facing Section

A — 500 · 501

B — 500 · 504 · 501 · cut 508 · 505

0   5 metres

Team Profile

Peter Bellamy – *Excavation Report Writer*

'When I was about eight years old I was introduced to an archaeological dig just up the road from where I lived. The diggers gave me a few pieces of Bronze Age pottery – nothing terribly special, but they were very important to me at the time and I still have them. Ever since then I had a yearning to make archaeology my career.

'I have been an archaeologist since 1976 and my favourite eras would have to be the Neolithic and Bronze Age periods because I like flint objects and enjoy the challenge of prehistory. I get very excited when I discover scatters of flint on the surface of fields because it generally gives you clues as to whether there was a prehistoric settlement there.

'The most time-consuming part of my job on *Time Team* is writing up sites after the digs. I am very concerned about keeping a proper archaeological record, including sketches and photographs, of everything we find in the trenches. Sorting through a pile of records on my own, putting them in order and making sure the site is finished after everyone else is long gone is probably the hardest, not to mention loneliest, part of my job.

'When I mention my involvement with the programme to my colleagues most of them are impressed and interested, while some consider it hard work. I would advise anyone contemplating a career as an archaeologist to go on a few digs before they decide, and perhaps try and do something allied to it – geology or conservation, for example. Archaeology is not well paid and there are few job prospects, but if you are the right person it is a wonderful thing to do. For me personally the chance to use my muscles and my head at the same time is very rewarding.'

Damian used a mixture of wool and tar to waterproof the planks – but just how to combine them was a problem. Was the wool dipped in the tar first? Or was the tar applied and the wool stuck on to it? We tried both methods. Dipping was expensive and wasted too much expensive tar, so we applied the tar first and then the wool, which gradually absorbed the tar.

A sketch of the structure was a useful prop and allowed viewers to see how small sections might have been assembled into a boat in the fourteenth and fifteenth centuries.

By the middle of Day Two John and Chris's extended search paid off and we found some archaeology at last: the remains of a slipway, a large area of brick rubble that may have been a kiln, a slip next to it and, finally, some ships' nails.

Stewart's search for lumps and bumps in the fields provided the first hint that there was a string of depressions that were possibly the surfaces of slips, and an aerial map showed a series of similar features. Could these be shipbuilding sites? We dug a new trench, Trench 4, towards the area of the medieval river channel and this produced a large area of sand. Although not exactly gripping from a visual point of view, it confirmed that sand had built up slowly at the water's edge. Large numbers of laminations or layers were visible in the section. It was these deposits that had finished the site off as a port. Run-off from land

Above: Getting in close to Damian Goodburn and Phil working on the cameo.

Above: Phil concentrates on the
final stages of the cameo.

reclaimed by farmers gradually silted up the river and prevented the
tides from clearing the estuary. The result was that by the early
seventeenth century only small ships could reach Smallhythe.

Ships require metalwork, tar and bricks – each of the galleons
would have had a brick fire-box – and one of our main goals was to see if
there were any traces in the area of the industries involved in providing
these. Dana Goodburn Brown, a metallurgist and Damian's partner, was
happy to provide an answer. We set her to work around two sites – Trench
5, which Phil was digging and which had revealed more of a brick
structure, and Trenches 6 and 7 which had been newly opened in the

fields behind Smallhythe Place. Dana's speciality is historical metalworking and she began by searching through piles of soil with a magnet. She was looking for two types of material: the splinters that break off heated metal when it is hammered on an anvil, and the metallic balls that are first seen as sparks when a red-hot bar of metal is hammered. The soil was damp and she had to dry it out first, which produced the rather strange sight of an archaeologist drying a spoil heap with a hairdryer.

Once collected, the small fragments were examined under a microscope and compared with material from the smithing we were doing back at the incident room. There was an exact match with the fragments from the trench behind Smallhythe Place. Once again this shows the advantage of skilled workers reproducing historical activities on site. The metal Dana had discovered proved that metalworking had taken place on the site.

The relative lack of activity in the delft area gave me a chance to enjoy one of my favourite *Time Team* activities: sitting on the side of Phil's trench. His forensic skill with his trowel is based on years of experience and over the several years I have watched him I have learned invaluable lessons in how archaeologists work, and why they dig a trench in a particular way. Just listening to Phil talk through the reality of the kinds of material he is digging gives an idea of how his perception works. There was a variation in the soil around the brick structure in the main trench. Phil commented: 'You can see that the dirt is a different colour from the dirt outside the brick area – it's darker and as you tap it, it feels solid like it was built in place.' His initial perception changes as he begins to work out the logic of the trench from the different textures and densities of the material in front of him.

I have learnt from listening to this kind of dialogue that the process of understanding a trench takes time, and that the archaeology needs to be analysed layer by layer. Each one provides a context and the finds in that context may help to date the layer. If an excavator is certain that a layer lies completely over the top of a section, it may suggest that it is later than the section. This can be critical to trying to understand the archaeology.

Archaeologists always avoid plucking a find from a layer or context because it could have its origins in a lower layer and this may be the only thing that dates the layer above it. Another concern, often expressed by excavators on *Time Team*, is the need to avoid treading on a surface that has been cleaned – the final stage in revealing a layer or context. This is the moment when subtle differences may appear in the surface and need to be recorded. Recording can mean drawing a complete and detailed view of the trench and I have to be patient while this is done. Watching a digger carefully draw bits of brick or pot and record them on a gridded surface requires Zen-like patience. It is not a

Below: Tony keeps the viewers informed with another key PTC. Nick Dance captures the moment.

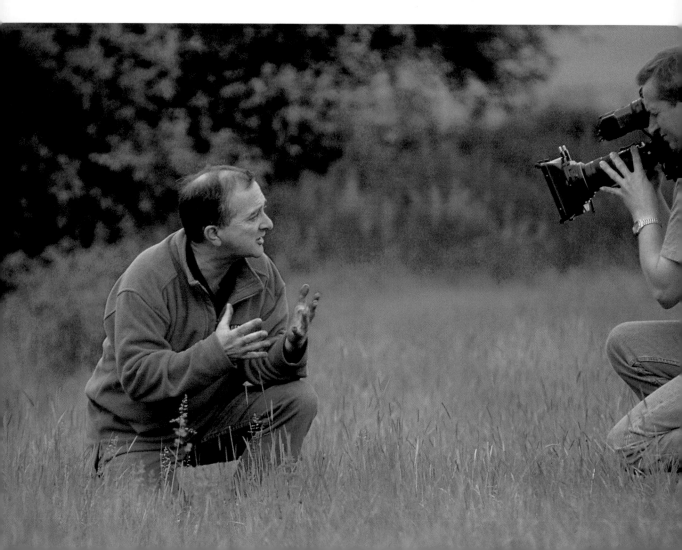

gripping process from the point of view of the director – in this case Alex West – but it has to be done. Until the archaeological recording is complete we cannot go into a deeper layer.

It can take hours of hard work to complete this final stage and Tony and the crew have learned to always ask the diggers' permission before treading in a trench. Once cleared, the layer can be photographed and if necessary we move on to the next one. It is an interesting moment when a layer that Phil has been protecting like a doting mother is removed to see what lies beneath it.

At Smallhythe the key finds we were searching for were ships' nails and these gradually began to emerge from the edge of Phil's Trench 5. Some appeared to be unused and others were badly corroded. Carenza had begun to clear out the pond in the fields adjoining Smallhythe Place but the material that came from it contained modern debris and lacked nails. It looked as though another

potential dockyard site had been knocked on the head. However, we now had geophysics data from this area and there were some hot spots (the site of Trench 6). Mick Worthington joined Carenza to investigate these and their initial investigations produced a kettle. More work would be needed on Day Three.

On the second night of the dig there was an interesting *Time Team* moment: 'the turnaround'. At the end of a long day, although everyone has stopped working and concentrating on the site, conversations continue and people get the chance to exchange views and ideas.

A conclave of experts gathered in the bar of the Ashford International Hotel and a new idea emerged. Gustav Milne had been reflecting on the wood we had found in the delft trenches. What if it wasn't prehistoric? Maybe it was more recent. Had boats been beached rather than built in the area where we been digging? Might boats have been dismantled there? Had it been a backwater wreckers' yard? If a shallow bay had existed at

Behind the Scenes at *Time Team*

Above: *Dana Goodburn compares the small fragments collected from the site with fragments taken from our smithing reconstruction work. Amazingly they matched, despite being 400 years older.*

the edges of the delft field this might provide an answer to these questions. We would have to return to the dig and see. The obvious solution – getting the wood carbon-dated – was just not available within *Time Team*'s three days.

On Day Three, to determine whether a bay existed, we ran a line of core samples up to the edge of the delft field to see if, for example, they showed the profile of an inlet. They didn't, and instead showed a gradually shelving beach which would have been too shallow to accommodate large vessels. Although it couldn't have been for shipbuilding, the exercise was very important in defining the limits of shipbuilding activity. However, we did make further progress in Carenza's field and Trench 6. She began to find a line of ships' nails within the outline of a boat-shaped depression below the kettle. Mick Aston was a little sceptical, but further work and Carenza's explanation – she can be very persuasive – finally convinced him. As we excavated deeper, the shape that held the nails took on the appearance of a small boat that had perhaps been used to reinforce the river bank.

A plus was
the Rother. Jane
fantastic job of sh
this series, in Coc
with very valuab
surprise because
ground or explod
hope to use it aga
entirely different
produce the same
the different layer
that will enable fu

Conclusion

Although we l
disappointment,
done, two mon
picture. He had
uncovered to the

Trench 6 had a sequel. It is amazing how often a final piece of evidence appears the day after a *Time Team* shoot, when the cameras have gone and the trenches are being finally recorded and backfilled. In this case we found a section of boat similar to the one Damian had constructed. We are in a dilemma when this happens. The temptation is to include the find in some kind of postscript, but by and large we don't do this. *Time Team* keeps to its three-day structure. On one occasion – a programme at Launceston, Cornwall – we gave the carbon-14 dating for a skeleton we had found on the site of a leper colony because it was critical to our interpretation of the site, but this is a rare example.

The slipway in Phil's Trench 5 also provided a satisfactory conclusion, while the brickwork turned out to be a kiln, possibly used to fire bricks, and part of a small industrial area alongside the shipbuilding site.

Although Smallhythe had many enjoyable elements it left me feeling slightly dissatisfied. In retrospect, it felt like a programme that we got strategically wrong. It exposed the problems of doing archaeology in three days. It is difficult to sort a site out if your initial hypothesis – in this case our focus on an enclosed dockyard – is

Below: Even after a long day the chat still keeps going. Brendan Hughes, the second unit director, talks through ideas with Alex West, Mick Worthington and assistant producer Tory Batten.

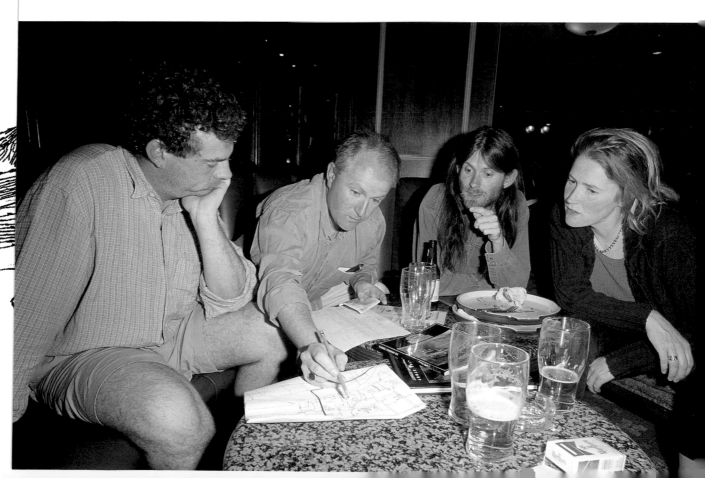

Above: Phil applyi
trowel. The bucket
foreground contai

Opposite: Victor's
Robin Bush who w
sample the produ
vineyard.

and told us that our work had located a site of international importance in the world of medieval shipbuilding! We had found a set of slipways and associated deposits that, possibly for the first time, gave a detailed picture of a shipbuilding site from the Middle Ages.

The key pieces of evidence were the nails. Of the 160 we had recovered, 100 were usable fragments, many with their nail head and rove which enabled us to estimate the size of the ships that were built or recycled at Smallhythe. The gap between the head and the rove indicates the thickness of the two pieces of timber in the clinker construction method. The larger the gap, the thicker the planks and therefore the larger the vessel. Thanks to the work of Professor Sean McGrail, we are able to estimate the size of the vessels at Smallhythe. The evidence suggests the presence of ships over twenty-five metres (seventy-five feet) long.

Large clinker-built ships were first built in about 1200 and were phased out around 1500 when the 'carvel' method of shipbuilding where planks were butted edge-to-edge was first introduced. This clearly helps to date our material.

The combination of the nail evidence and the location of slipways found by Stewart and excavated during the programme, has led Gustav to refer to Smallhythe as *the* fossil for medieval shipbuilding for the period prior to the royal dockyards at Chatham in Kent. He is particularly pleased that the site has helped to correct the image of medieval shipbuilding sites as being made up of docks and quays and describes Smallhythe as a record of the final days of the great clinker-built ships.

Smallhythe has now been considered important enough for the Institute of Archaeology to set up the Smallhythe Interpretation Project, which goes under the appropriate acronym SHIP. Work, including examination of the composition of the nails and of the whole range of finds, is to continue on the site.

Below: Tony with Nancy Duin, Channel 4's editorial consultant, talking to local school-children about our finds. Wherever possible we try to keep our sites open for visits from local people.

Following page: These rather crusty looking objects turned out to hold some crucial clues to the site. Some even have the diamond-shaped rove attached.

CHAPTER 5

Reedham Marshes, Norfolk

TONY'S PIECE TO CAMERA: 'Just over fifty years ago, this tranquil Norfolk fenland was the scene of a tragic, and unsolved, wartime mystery. It was February 1944, and in the sky above 300 American bombers were returning from a mission over Germany. Minutes away from the safety of base, one of the bombers suddenly collided with another and the two aircraft plummeted to earth somewhere here in Reedham Marshes. All twenty-one crew were killed. So what happened? ... We'll be excavating one of the planes, in the hope its carcass may yield some clues; and we'll be trying to find out as much as we can about the two crews, and the sequence of events that led to the crash.'

Opposite: *Start them young – a junior helper gets stuck in to a spoil heap at the edge of the site.*

Above: *The opening night and a lot of experts have come to spread their accumulated wisdom.*

The Battle in the Air

American airmen were vital to the defence of Britain during the Second World War. The first squadrons arrived in July 1942 and at the height of the conflict more than 1,000 aeroplanes and 200,000 aircrew and support staff were involved in the war against Germany. They flew daylight bombing raids against industrial targets and provided fighter escorts.

Destroying the German war machine was a primary objective. Factories making engines, ball bearings or synthetic rubber and oil refineries were key targets. The accuracy possible by flying in daylight was a major strategic advantage but made the bombers more vulnerable to attack. The B–17s expected to get over 407 of their bombs within five hundred metres (1666 feet) of their target. On some of the missions over three hundred planes would be committed.

The Japanese attack on Pearl Harbour in 1941 made America increase its military capacity. Boeing at Seattle in Washington was the main production centre for B-17s which along with the B-24 Liberators were the main bombers.

The key fighters were the P–47 Thunderbolts, P–38 Lightnings and, perhaps the most famous of all, P–51 Mustangs. The latter were capable of long-distance fighter support but came into use relatively late into the war. The B–17 had a formidable defensive armoury of machine guns and could carry a massive bomb load of over 19,800 kilogrammes (9,000 pounds). It was so successful that more than 12,000 had been built by the end of the war. The B–17G, which had a chin turret beneath its nose, was the main model. It arrived in Britain in September 1943 and pilots loved it because it flew like a smaller plane and its strong structure meant it could survive damage more easily. The 'Memphis Belle', star of the eponymous film, was a B–17G. The original 'Memphis Belle' was one of the first planes to complete twenty-five missions. Crews that had completed this number were allowed to return to the USA.

The strategy of daylight bombing depended on 'group integrity', large numbers of planes flying in tight formation, allowing concentrated fire power from their collective multiple turrets.

Behind the Scenes at *Time Team*

Rounds from these guns would be scattered across a wide area in the vicinity of the crash site, and would be one of the key pieces of evidence we would find during the dig. A B–17 would often carry up to 25,000 rounds of ammunition.

It has been estimated that by the end of the Second World War approximately 640,000 tons of bombs had been dropped by B–17s. Losses to aircrew were heavy: in October 1943 sixty bombers out of 229 failed to return from a raid. More than 50,000 American personnel were killed or listed as missing in action, and it was not often that an entire crew survived to achieve the twenty-five missions that gave them their tickets home. Most of the airmen were youngsters: the average age was just twenty-two years.

During the programme we didn't get chance to refer to the names of all the members of the crews of the two planes that crashed at Battle. The final crew lists were as follows.

First Lieutenant Warren J. Pease's crew (549th Bomb Squadron): First Lieutenant Warren J. Pease (pilot), Second Lieutenant Edward B. Brown (co-pilot), Second Lieutenant Bernard Kaplan (navigator), Second Lieutenant Robert E. Jenkins (bombardier), Technical Sergeant William R. Clift (top turret), Technical Sergeant William Gill Jr (radio operator), Staff Sergeant Franklin C. Owsley (ball turret), Staff Sergeant Junior M. Falls (tail gunner), Staff Sergeant Harold E. Dickason (left waist gunner) and Staff Sergeant Gail F. Bruner (right waist gunner).

Captain John N. Hutchison's crew (550th Bomb Squadron): Captain John N. Hutchison (pilot), Second Lieutenant Charles G. Curtis (co-pilot), First Lieutenant John E. Epps (navigator), First Lieutenant Edmond J. Gamble (bombardier), Technical Sergeant Roy C. Kitner (top turret), Staff Sergeant Joseph J. Carpinetti (tail gunner), Technical Sergeant William J. Dukes (radio operator), Staff Sergeant John H. Erhardt (ball turret), Staff Sergeant Emilio M. Corgnatti (left waist gunner), Staff Sergeant Peter Bobulsky Jr (right waist gunner) and Staff Sergeant Frank L. Creegan (photographer).

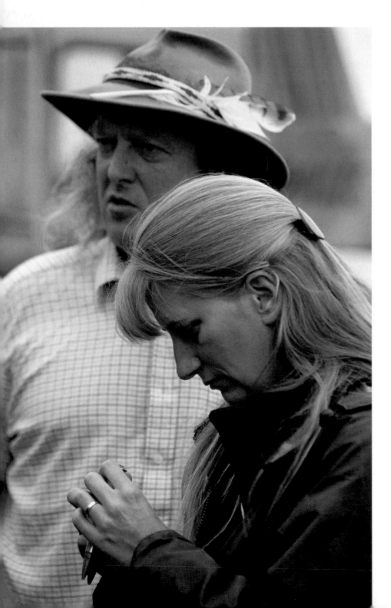

When the experts at the meeting on the night before we started to shoot the programme we had come to call 'Bombers' included a bomb-disposal crew, an air-crash investigator, an environmental policeman from English Nature, a team of civil engineers and assorted aeroplane enthusiasts we knew we were in for an interesting weekend. Over fifty people were crowded into the stuffy hotel room when I arrived for the opening briefing. The tragic facts behind the programme were clear. Two B–17s of the United States Army Air Force had collided on their return from a mission in February 1944 during the Second World War and both crews, twenty-one men, had been killed. We were to search for the wreckage of one of the planes buried in Norfolk peat, and see what we could add to the information about the causes of the crash.

At the front of the room the flight sergeant from bomb disposal was well into his stride describing the lethal potential of a Browning 0.50 inch machine-gun round with a clarity that drew the blood from Carenza's face and had Phil making a strange sound that I have come to recognize over the years – something between a hysterical giggle and a long-drawn-out 'Errr...' The fact that over 6,000 of these rounds might be scattered around the crash site concentrated everyone's attention.

Work on 'Bombers' had begun to get complicated two months earlier. A series of events was triggered by the somewhat late identification of the area of the crash as a Site of Special Scientific Interest. SSSIs are notified under the Wildlife and Countryside Act 1981, in recognition of their special biological and/or geological interest. Notification has to be given to English Nature before specified activities can be carried out on the sites, in part to reduce the hostility to wildlife of the surrounding land and protect the quality of the water and air environments. Whatever we did in the area would also have to be cleared by the Environment Agency.

To get clearance to work on a vulnerable and protected site we had to define the size of the trench or trenches we wanted to dig and get the area they would cover surveyed beforehand. Exact dimensions were unclear at this stage because we could not tell precisely where and how the plane had crashed. The bigger the trench, the bigger the bill for the survey. The cost of a survey that would cover every potential excavation area might be so high that it would prevent the programme going ahead at all. It seemed appropriate that on this particular excavation we were facing an element of catch-22.

I had always thought that 'Bombers' would be an exciting programme. It would show archaeology being applied to a new and different subject for *Time Team* and in that sense would be 'educational' for viewers. And we all felt that the potential difficulties would produce a classic *Time Team* struggle against the odds – one of the elements of a more interesting programme – with, hopefully, a successful conclusion. Sites that appear to have a direct and easy route to a predictable outcome do not have the right feel for the series.

Above: *Water from our excavation had to be drained into an artificial pond. Local engineers, Mules Engineering, helped to create the structure to deal with the problems we faced.*

Following page: *Pictures of members of B–17 crews. The site generated masses of ephemera and technical manuals.*

Team Profile

Nick Dance – *Lighting Cameraman*

'I have worked on *Time Team* since the very first shoot, which was the hunt for a Norman feasting hall at Much Wenlock in Shropshire. Over the past six years I have shot eighty per cent of the programmes and of all the digs I have covered I particularly enjoyed St Mary's City in Maryland, USA, because of the beauty of the location. However, Sanday on the Orkneys holds very fond memories. We arrived to terrible weather but by the next day we were blessed with Mediterranean blue skies, and long days of sunshine – a very rare occurrence up there. Because of the geographical position of the Orkneys the light was fantastic and stayed that way until late into the evening.

'*Time Team* is a very spontaneous programme and as a lighting cameraman I have to be ready to capture the moment as it happens. Being aware of what is going on and trying to get the shot in one take is essential to convey the essence of a dig. I use a Beta SP video camera (BBW400), which is a broadcast betacam system, normally with a wide-angle lens. I have become very used to the camera on my shoulder, to the point where it has almost become an extension of my arm. I imagine that cameras will get smaller and smaller in the future, although I am dubious as to how small they can get without the quality being affected. I think the tiny DVcams are rather more suited to home movies than television and to my mind it would be better if the weight rather than the size of the camera were reduced as size helps with stability.

'One way or another there are, of course, problems on all the shoots but 'Bombers' was a dangerous dig because of the size of the hole needed to excavate the plane. Getting close to the edge to get the picture also increased the possibility of falling in! Greylake on the Somerset Levels was a 'technically' difficult shoot because we were digging into very dark peat while contending with very bright sunshine, which created problems with exposure. Variable weather also tends to be another major headache, especially when it rains. The Islay site was the worst for wet weather. I had been in Cairo just before the dig, with temperatures reaching ninety degrees and beyond. When I flew into Islay it was freezing despite being summer. Tim kept our spirits up with an endless supply of Islay Malt! I think you have to be prepared for anything and everything on *Time Team*.'

At one stage, however, it seemed likely that the programme would never get started. We had already delayed the shoot and moved it from early spring – a time that a local contact told us would be 'ideal' (it wasn't) – to early summer; and Simon Raikes, the director, and I had numerous meetings to reassure ourselves that the programme was a go-er, only to be hit by one hitch after another. One thing that kept us going was the endless stream of excellent information that the researchers managed to uncover, much of it provided by contacts in the United States and Ian McLachlan, the aviation archaeologist who had suggested the site to us and whose book *Final Flights* was a goldmine of information. After a depressing morning reading the likely costs of an environmental survey we received a package from America that contained colour film, complete with soundtrack, of a B–17 bomber under attack by Messerschmitt 109s. The production office became quiet as we saw the film and listened to men talking, and then shouting warnings to each other as they fought for their lives.

From the start one of our main concerns was that the site was a place where men like these had died. Officially we had obtained the correct permissions to excavate a crash site and knew all the bodies had been removed in the months after the crash, but in the back of everyone's mind was the thought that it was possible that not all the remains had been removed from the wreckage.

I was concerned that we should respect this element, but also felt that if the living relatives were in agreement and we received the right advice from the Ministry of Defence, which protects crash sites with strict licensing, we should go ahead. There was a possibility that the inevitable and understandable sadness associated with the site would dominate the programme. However, the feeling was that we would be able to clear up the mystery of the crash so that the site could, in the words of Ian Mclachlan, 'be laid to rest', and that this ought to prevail.

As the date of possible filming came nearer, the environmental issues that a survey had to address became clearer. The fact that a television programme is being made and will be broadcast to millions tends to make officials additionally careful that they are seen to be doing the right thing. The key factor was that a deep excavation could release contaminated water into surface watercourses and threaten farmland and animals' drinking water. At depth, contamination could be caused by fuel and oil from the plane or by chemicals created by the decomposition of plant material. The bigger the hole the more likely it

Behind the Scenes at *Time Team*

was that the water had been contaminated. A B–17 is over a twenty-four metres (seventy-four feet) long with a wingspan of nearly thirty-five metres (104 feet). Many of our discussions had centred on whether or not we would be able to find enough of the wreck to come to a conclusion as to why it had crashed. We had contacted an air-crash investigator who had indicated that he would need to see key parts of the plane such as the engines, propellers and cockpit. Finding these might require a huge trench.

At this stage money was becoming a critical issue. Each programme has a set budget and over a series we expect that some will be a bit more expensive and others a little cheaper and that the costs will balance out overall. However, a programme that goes badly over-budget can jeopardize others in the series. Zarina Dick, the production manager, talked to surveyors and engineering companies; a deep hole would require specialist digging machines, but until we had defined the size of the dig and a survey had taken place it was difficult to put an exact figure on the likely overspend. The awful possibility arose that we might spend thousands of pounds on a complex survey only to come up with such a negative report that we would not be able to go ahead.

By March we had taken the plunge and the survey went ahead. We all kept a worried eye on the proceedings as highly qualified environmental scientists plumbed the depths of the Norfolk peat. When the results finally appeared they gave us the all clear with certain reservations. We would have to create pools to hold the water so that its quality could be checked, and make a careful plan to ensure that the peat and clay layers were replaced correctly. The report made clear the potentially hazardous nature of the environment with which we would be dealing. An interpretation of the technical jargon revealed that there was what appeared to be a 1.2 metre (four feet) layer of peat, a layer of clay of varying thickness and beneath this a material that, with the addition of water, would turn into chocolate mousse and whose depth could be in excess of five metres (fifteen feet) – potentially lethal to anyone who fell into it. An interesting duet continued all through March and April: bits of fascinating information on the planes accompanied by worrying environmental details – and the occasional dull thud of a bill for heavy engineering plant. By the end of April we were looking at costs in excess of several thousand pounds and had not shot an inch of tape.

During this time we gradually got to know our punters better. They ranged from enthusiasts with some detailed skills and knowledge

Opposite top: *After scraping for hours in an attempt to lever up a bakelite panel with his trowel, Phil finally decided that a shovel was the best tool to lift the piece intact.*

Opposite bottom: *Embarrassed by what appeared to be a somewhat crude choice of implement Mr Harding prefers anonymity. While he is distracted I take the opportunity to have a quick scrape.*

Above: *Jenni Butterworth records a key area in the main trench. The hoses are already in action.*

experts, Tim Chittock and Vic Doughty, who had dug channels in peat before. They were to prove invaluable over the three days of the shoot.

As the first bucket load came out of Trench 1 we saw how unstable the area was. Each movement of a mechanical digger made the entire ground surface wobble like a large jelly. The other reality that soon became apparent was that the enthusiasm of our local helpers would have to be tempered. As each bucket of peat emerged an army of them descended, metal detectors in hand, to look for finds. Some of them wanted to pluck bits out of the trench. There were safety implications: we were not sure how deep or strong the layer of peat was and whether it could support a person's weight.

Entry into the dig had to be carefully controlled and in time this affected the way *Time Team* excavators recorded finds. There were occasions when it looked simply too dangerous for a digger to get into the trench and we had to rely on the skills of Tim and Vic to extract material mechanically, and then examine it away from the crumbling edges of the trench. Alex Cox, the production supervisor, and I had read

Team Profile

Ian Powesland – *Digger*

'Working on Second World War sites is not just about archaeology, it is also part of the personal history of my family and many other people I have known over the years. This was brought home to me while I was cleaning the peat from the fragments of the B-17 and the burnt olive paint that was revealed was as fresh as it had been on the day of the crash. I hope we treated the site with the respect it deserves.

'I always had an interest in history as a child, probably because my parents dragged me round lots of old castles in the West Country which is full of hill-forts. I did a Higher National Diploma in practical archaeology in Yeovil in 1992 and then became a professional archaeologist. A particularly memorable moment came early in my career. I was taking a stroll along the ramparts in Battlesbury near Warminster when I discovered half the top of a Middle Iron Age pot, about six to seven inches wide, sticking out of Badger's hole. It was an exciting find because it was such a surprise.

'I am currently a researcher at Bristol University and work as a digger on *Time Team*. The most difficult part of my job on the programme is keeping calm because things can be very hectic and unexpected at times. Of all the digs I think my favourite would have to be the Roman site at Papcastle in Cumbria, as Roman and prehistoric periods are my speciality. It was also a classic *Time Team* from the point of view of going into someone's back garden and digging up historical finds. When I mention to my colleagues that I work on the programme the response varies because, in some ways, *Time Team* is unlike most archaeological jobs as it is so fast and not really average bread-and-butter archaeology. I would recommend an HND in practical archaeology to someone who wanted to become a professional archaeologist because it provides such a good grounding. The training helped to open lots of doors for me.

'Field survey is my particular speciality. Every time I walk into a field or farm that I have never surveyed before and find earthworks and lumps and bumps I really enjoy the process of sketching and planning them in order to try and work out what they are. I also love finding things that nobody has ever found before or, as is frequently the case, bothered to notice!'

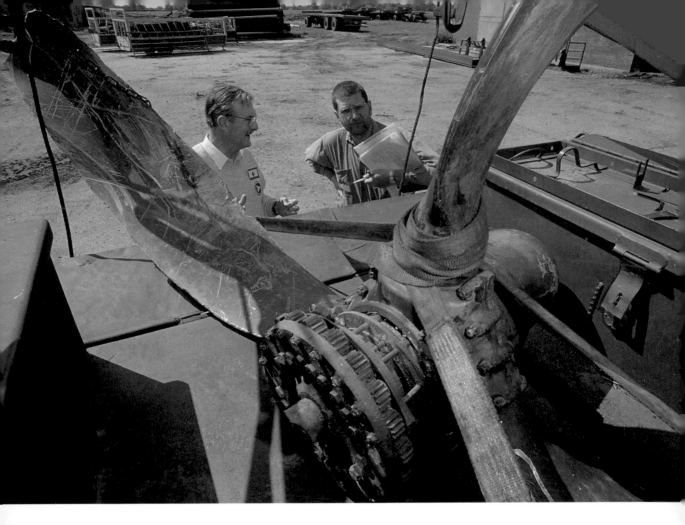

*Above: Air crash investigator
Bernie Ford with Stewart
examining the propeller blades
from the B17. It was the position
of the blades and their condition
that suggested a vital clue to the
cause of the crash.*

the health and safety document for the excavation and were well aware
of our responsibilities if an accident occurred. With digger buckets of
huge dimensions in operation and the trench growing deeper, safety
became a major consideration.

Mick, Phil and I insisted that, where possible, we should treat the
site of the crash as we would that of any other archaeological
investigation. Finds would be recorded in their context or layer and
Bernard Thomason would map their location exactly with a theodolite.
This would provide some idea of their distribution which might yield
clues to how the plane was lying. The team gradually settled into this
way of working.

By lunchtime we had begun to locate our first pieces of plane and
quantities of machine-gun rounds in Trench 2. Our local helpers told us
that the reddish stain they caused in the peat was typical and this made
them fairly easy to spot. The RAF bomb-disposal team moved into
action as each round appeared to check its condition and make it safe.

Many had lost their bullets or were damaged. A few were complete. Although a round would detonate only if its end was struck precisely with a sharp object, and the damp conditions meant that the main charge was no longer viable, we took careful precautions with each one.

We had also begun to find pieces of crumpled aircraft and it was now that one of our key experts came into action. Bob Spangler had been a master sergeant on a local USAF airbase during the war and had been in charge of maintaining the B–17s. Now resident in the United States he had returned to Norfolk to identify the pieces as they appeared. The bits of plane accumulated gradually and were washed down and laid out for Bob's perusal. He would contemplate a screwed-up mass of metal and say: 'Yes, it's part of the lower wing assembly near the Tokyo tanks. We called them that because they were supposed to carry the extra fuel needed to bomb Japan.' This kind of detail was critical and made me think how experts from the past would have been equally helpful if we could have brought them to life. To hear a medieval shipbuilder talk about his trade or a Roman smith describe how he made iron would have provided a wonderful insight. Bob's contribution to the programme demonstrated the value of getting as close as possible to the people who have the skills needed to construct the objects we

Below: Despite the violence of the crash some fragile objects like this wing-tip navigation light had survived intact.

excavate. No one knows a machine as well as the person who has had to make or maintain it.

The crash investigator would soon be able to make his initial judgements, but by the end of Day One none of the critical pieces of plane had been found and John and Sue's geophysics had produced no sign of a big response that could be the engines.

As Day Two got under way I became increasingly concerned that we hadn't resolved a key problem: the exact location of the main crash and the angle of dive of the plane as it entered the peat. Stewart believed that it had plunged down vertically, probably into the part of the site now occupied by a dyke but nothing appeared when we began to delve into that area with the mechanical digger's longest extension arm. The alternative possibility was that the plane had come in at a shallow angle and belly flopped, travelling along the ground and scattering wreckage far and wide. There were odd ambiguities in some of the remains. Two glass navigation lights remained intact – would these have survived a massive vertical impact?

Back at the 'Bombers' site we were relying on three pieces of information to give us an idea of the crash location: an aerial photograph of what seemed to be the wreckage and showed an area that could be roughly identified because woods that had been there in 1944 still existed; and eyewitness reports and colour photographs from an earlier dig that had located the propeller. Using all three, Stewart and Mick made their best guess as to the epicentre of the crash. However, there was no response when we searched the area with geophysics.

Day Three at last began to produce the significant finds we had hoped for, but the location of the engines and the main fuselage remains a mystery. From Trench 2, our main trench, we had already retrieved fragments of cockpit glass and personal items that brought home the reality of the crash. These included parachute harnesses, a piece of a flying cap, a pilot's boot, a glove and the armed back of the pilot's seat.

We began to use all our geophysics and metal detectors in unison, getting each of them to crosscheck each response. John and his team scanned the surfaces of both trenches and as we got lower in the excavations we asked the RAF team to use their detecting gear to go over the same areas. We followed a significant response in Trench 2 and up

Below: *Stewart Ainsworth using the photographs to suggest a possible location for the crash.*

Following page: *The broad Norfolk landscape with its dykes and fens had preserved the secrets of the crash for fifty years. The dimensions of the main trench would set us a series of major civil-engineering challenges.*

explosion. The RAF team went into action and, at a site 200 metres (600 feet) away, set off a very impressive explosion. The detonator was pressed by Professor Aston on the occasion of his birthday.

We laid out all our finds on the ground and, with the help of Bob Spangler and Bernie Ford, the air-crash investigator, located each piece in the approximate position it would have occupied in the aircraft.

Conclusion

It is probably appropriate to end with two pieces of information. The first is that the men who died never had a memorial and that large pieces of the B–17 and one of the two machine guns will be used to create one. The second is Bernie Ford's crash report reprinted on page 181 the dry analytical facts behind which we all felt the presence of the young aircrew who gave their lives in the Second World War.

Opposite: The bomb-disposal crew from RAF Wittering – with just a fraction of the machine-gun rounds found on the site.

Below: Hosing down the Browning machine gun. A live round was later found in the breach.

B–17 Site, Reedham Marsh, June/July 1998

The Air-Crash Investigator Report – Bernie Ford

'The probable sequence of events was as follows. Three B–17s entered cloud on their descent. At some time the No. 2 (Pease) left the formation. This may have been due to an engine failure because one propeller was found in the feathered 1 position, i.e. the condition that the pilot would select following an engine failure. The distraction caused by this emergency may have led the pilot to become disorientated. The aircraft was seen by the other members of the formation to come out of cloud in a steep dive at high speed. It passed below the other two aircraft and then executed a vigorous pull-out, which led it to fly in front of the leader. In the subsequent collision, at about 800 feet, the entire tail unit (aft of the waist gunmen) was severed. The aircraft continued to climb for a short period before falling back into the lead aircraft. This collision caused the lead aircraft to break in two. Evidence for this is from eyewitnesses in the No. 3 aircraft and also damage to the second propeller from the No. 2 aircraft indicating that it had hit something round and very solid, possibly a gun. The No. 2 aircraft then fell at an angle close to the vertical and crashed into a drainage ditch at an estimated speed of about 200 mph. This estimate of speed is from extensive experience of the state of the wreckage where the impact speed was known.'

Previous page: *Professor Aston's birthday present goes up in smoke – a satisfactory conclusion to the dig.*

Opposite: *Sue Francis takes digital still of the crash wreckage – cameraman Dennis Borrow and soundman Doug Dredger capture the moment.*

Following page: *The end of the 'Bombers' shoot. Relief and elation were mixed in equal measure. Simon Raikes, Brendan Hughes and myself couldn't resist getting our hands on the machine guns. The cameo piece of nose artwork in the background made a perfect backdrop.*

The Final Cut

Hopefully, by the time I see the first edit of a programme I will be able to look at it objectively.

Philip Clarke, the executive producer, and I were viewing the Beauport Park programme with the director, Graham Dixon, and editor, Michael Pike.

For the director and editor this is the penultimate stage in a long process that is critical to the way a programme works on the screen. Graham had started with forty-two videotapes from the shoot – approximately twenty-one hours of material which had to be cut down to fifty minutes or so. Most *Time Team* directors shoot between thirty-seven and forty tapes per programme. They have two weeks to view them on VHS and make an initial selection. All the tapes are logged – this is not done on the shoot – and the best bits are selected and the worst ones rejected. The off-line process takes three weeks including a final week to view the programme and make any changes, and we then go to Channel 4 with what we hope will be something close to the final version. When it has been approved it is on-lined and Tony reads the voice-over. Graphics and a finalized version of the 'big picture', as we call it, are put in by Sue Francis and Steve Breeze.

At the initial viewing the director has tapes that show time-code numbers on the screen – the ten-digit code enables the editor to locate exact points on the original tape. We off-line on Avid digital edit machines, which store the edit on disk. Storage is expensive and therefore limited. Four and a half hours of programme can be stored on nine gigabytes of memory at medium resolution. We normally have eighteen gigabytes, which means that the director will try to reduce the material down to eight hours or so by the time the off-line starts.

Editing sessions always make me recall the first series of *Time Team* and the pilot programme which saw Graham and I editing on tape in a dodgy hotel to save money and so that he could be near his home. Tape editing involves spending ages waiting for the tape machines to roll to the right editing point, which means shifting up and down a thirty-minute tape. It also restricts your ability to look at different versions of the programme easily. With digital editing it is easy to extract a sequence and change its position or put it together in a different way, much as text is cut and pasted on a personal computer. Graham was editing Beauport Park on an Avid film composer with twenty-seven gigabytes of memory and in his initial viewing had been able to edit down to approximately thirteen hours of tape. It is easy to remove a section of material, put it aside for possible future use and replace it with another, but most directors try to store all the material they will need at an early stage. Hard choices have to be made from the start and in the case of Beauport Park there was a lack of clear archaeological results for the first two days.

Graham had decided to edit together a set of key sequences from Day One to be sure of keeping them and then went to Day Three when the main archaeological finds had been made. He also edited the cameo. We both wanted this to play an important role in the programme and, to an extent, make up for the realities of the archaeology. With these key islands in place he went on to edit the first Day Two material around them.

The dialogue in an editing suite is aimed at providing an objective response to the programme and giving the director ideas about any changes that need to be made before it is shown to Channel 4. He reads the voice-over at this stage and we are usually given a script before the viewing starts. When Tony does the final voice-over it is amazing the difference it makes to the final programme, and he will change bits of the content to suit his delivery. We have had enough experience to predict what he will feel comfortable with and in the editing suite we concentrate on whether the programme tells its story clearly. The dialogue that follows gives an idea of the kind of discussion that went on around Beauport Park.

Tim: When you go into Stewart's trench you get slightly lost as to which one it is of the three.

Graham: I'll make that clearer on the graphics.

Phil: I think there is a problem with the end of Day Two when Mick and Phil Harding say they have looked in lots of places but we don't see any of the cutting back of forest to which they are referring in the first half. There is also a sequence in the same day that I think should be dropped – again to do with how far did we look and how did we work? I think the sequence when we are looking in the pits full of black water should be included to generate the feeling of a hunt.

Graham: The problem was that you couldn't really see it because it was so dark, so it didn't really translate on tape.

Tim: When Stewart appears looking in the stream we need to make the context of the scene clear.

Graham: Yes I agree. I don't think we have fully worked this one out yet.

Tim: I would like some commentary and then a shot of Stewart still chopping away at the wood. This was a physically hard moment in the excavation, and a close-up of someone struggling with a branch might illustrate the reality of the moment. We need one of those classic shots of Stewart wandering around in hot pursuit of clues of 'activity'.

Above: *The final film is on-lined. Graham Dixon, in the sepulchral gloom of an edit suite, puts in the finishing touches.*

Graham: There are loads of shots of Stewart I could include.

Tim: The other thing that you must define is the reason we see a dog dashing around every so often on the site!

Graham: The dog is a pet belonging to one of the diggers. He travels everywhere with her.

Our key feeling was that the programme worked and achieved a good balance between the reality of the archaeology, the enjoyment of the cameo and the content of the trenches. From the start Graham had intended to use the golf as a humorous counterpoint to the archaeology and this worked well. Phil did an excellent job as our eye into the cameo and the final sequences in which the metal was produced were great. We

Behind the Scenes at *Time Team*

needed more of a sensation of struggling in the early scenes and some clearing up of trench numbers – but in general we both felt that the programme worked and did the classic *Time Team* job of realistically facing up to a difficult site and making the process enjoyable.

There were some hard decisions along the way – bits of film we had to leave out. This is inevitable. Some of Victor Ambrus's drawings, for example, were excellent but featured material that we had not found and therefore seemed out of place. We had not addressed the way the site had been handled previously or the issue of local helpers using divining rods. There is a point when you have to go with the director's vision, which creates a programme that has its own reality. This is the nature of a combined creative process.

Epilogue

When I think back over the programmes featured in this book each one evokes strong memories and images of what we achieved. The cavers and diggers at Cooper's Hole covered in mud and hauling up their improvised sled full of material from deep inside the cave. The mass of pottery falling from the digger bucket in Burslem and the hundreds of friendly faces that watched it happen. The weight of the machine guns from the trenches on the 'Bombers' shoot. The sparks flying from ships' nails as they were hammered by the smith at Smallhythe. The trenches deep in the woods at Beauport Park and the final glint of sunlight on the piece of iron. Chris captured some of these moments and preserved them in his photographs.

It is difficult to say which was my favourite programme. Although we did not find a lot at Beauport Park the dig was a great example of the *Time Team* working through a hypothesis. It showed that an honest process can be interesting and that there is no need to find a body or gold dish to make archaeology interesting. I hope

Above: *Brendan Hughes taking a well-earned rest from the rigours of second unit directing.*

what comes across is that after forty programmes and seven years of working together all of us still enjoy the series and are thrilled when we somehow manage to pluck triumph from disaster.

It is worth emphasizing that each *Time Team* shoot is a unique piece of archaeology that will be an important addition to the archaeological record. It could provide the key to a particular puzzle that has existed for years. It is probably true to say that few of the excavations would have taken place if they hadn't been chosen and funded by a *Time Team* programme. In this sense we all feel proud of the fact that *Time Team* has made a considerable contribution to the historical record by investing in these sites, and that our work will be an invaluable source for the future.

Time Team is not just about the archaeology. Each programme is also a human drama about overcoming practical problems and keeping to a story-line that will ultimately carry viewers with it. It is a drama that often takes place away from the cameras, and I hope that when you see the photographs in this book and read how the programmes evolved you will feel that you have had a chance to eavesdrop on what goes on behind the scenes, and have an increased understanding of the archaeological techniques we use. I hope, too, that you will share in the excitement and elation the *Time Team* group still feels when, usually at the last moment, the evidence unfolds.

Above: *It's been a long year and sometimes we all need a bit of a lie down! Mr Robinson is probably dreaming of where he'll be heading next on* Time Team.

Acknowledgments

Tim Taylor and Chris Bennett would like to thank all of *Time Team* and its crew for the cooperation that made this book possible.

Particular thanks go to the following people, who checked specific details in the text:

Chapter 1: Andy Currant, Bob Smart and Bob Croft.

Chapter 2: Bill Klemperer and Noel Boothroyd.

Chapter 3: Guy de la Bédoyère.

Chapter 4: Gustav Milne and Ian Friel.

Chapter 5: Ian McLachlan.

With special thanks to Liz Warner, Time Team's current Commissioning Editor, for her support during these programmes.

Finally, with thanks to Karla Goodman for relentlessly pursuing all the contributors and collating additional information.